The Future of the MBA

The Future of the MBA ———

——— *Designing the Thinker of the Future*

Mihnea C. Moldoveanu and Roger L. Martin

OXFORD
UNIVERSITY PRESS
2008

OXFORD
UNIVERSITY PRESS

Oxford University Press, Inc., publishes works that further
Oxford University's objective of excellence
in research, scholarship, and education.

Oxford   New York
Auckland   Cape Town   Dar es Salaam   Hong Kong   Karachi
Kuala Lumpur   Madrid   Melbourne   Mexico City   Nairobi
New Delhi   Shanghai   Taipei   Toronto

With offices in
Argentina   Austria   Brazil   Chile   Czech Republic   France   Greece
Guatemala   Hungary   Italy   Japan   Poland   Portugal   Singapore
South Korea   Switzerland   Thailand   Turkey   Ukraine   Vietnam

Published by Oxford University Press, Inc.
198 Madison Avenue, New York, New York 10016

www.oup.com

Oxford is a registered trademark of Oxford University Press

Libraray of Congress Cataloging-in-Publication Data
Moldoveanu, Mihnea C.
The future of the MBA: designing the thinker of the future / Mihnea C.
Moldoveanu and Roger L. Martin.
    p. cm.
Include bibliographical references and index.
ISBN 978-0-19-534014-3
1. Master of business administration degree.   2. Business education
I. Martin, Roger L.   II. Title.
HF1111.M65 2007
650.071'1—dc22   2007021137

9   8   7   6   5   4   3   2

Printed in the United States of America
on acid-free paper

For Marcel Desautels and Joe Rotman

Acknowledgments of Debts,
Intellectual and Beyond

This book has been several years in gestation, but the spark that brought it to life was a conference—hosted by the authors at the Rotman School of Management in March 2006—entitled The Future of the MBA. The conference brought together deans from leading business schools around the world with articulate authors of recent critiques of the Master of Business Administration program and prominent academics representing the basic and applied fields of the social sciences represented in business academia. The conference was motivated by our intention to have critics of the MBA deliver their critiques directly *to* those in a position to do something about the substance of the critiques, with the ultimate aim of turning a series of potentially powerful but disconnected monologues into a connected dialogue, one that forms the basis and starting point of our own critique and reconstructive approach to the problem: *Does the MBA have a future? If so, then what should this future look like?*

"*Should*," not "*will*": for, implicit in the very notion of a reconstructive project is the belief that social phenomena do not follow deterministic trajectories—technological or otherwise—but, rather, are subjects of *design* and *engineering* rather than merely of *discovery* and *analysis*. As Michael Jensen put it to us all with a slightly menacing look, "If we are not about 'should,' then what in the world are we doing?"

On this view, logic itself—as we shall argue in the text you are about to read—is a well-designed tool for performing inquiry into the workings of natural, psychic, and social worlds, rather than a "given" and incorrigible or immutable set of rules, principles, or axioms. If it is the case—as

Ken Andrews once pointed out to one of us in private conversation—that "pragmatism is the philosophy of business," then it should not come as a surprise that the reconstructive project we have engaged in places itself comfortably in the intellectual lineage of pragmatist philosophers and (more importantly) thinkers that starts with Charles Peirce and William James, continues with John Dewey and the later Martin Heidegger, and continues with Richard Rorty and several of his students. The subtitle of our book—*Designing the Thinker of the Future*—is, then, both an exhortation *to* professional education programs (most prominently the MBA) to become *designers* of better thinkers, better communicators, better managers, better humans, and an acknowledgment of the fundamental design orientation of the educational reformer, who should aim to *design and build the designer* of more successful human interactions.

We start our design odyssey with an elaboration of parts of the dialogue which the meeting of minds in Toronto produced—a sign, we trust, that the words spoken there did not float past one another with the fleeting casualness that characterizes, we fear, much academic discourse. Whatever else it may be, dialogue is an engine for producing commitments, both discursive and behavioral, and is thus a crucial part of the development of ideas meant to become embodied in practice. The project that we have undertaken is not a purely theoretical exercise—even though "theory" is prominently on display throughout. Indeed, we have already embarked on the engineering and prototyping work required to bring our design to life, therefore many of the ideas of the book are already "alive" at the Rotman School of Management: they do real, causal work upon the complicated landscape of "an MBA education," supply interventions and blueprints for the development of new ways of being, and have become part of the everyday language in which we think and talk about the MBAs of the future. Indeed, we hope that those who gave of their minds, energy, and time to participate in our dialogical sessions in Toronto will find some measure of satisfaction in our attempt to integrate their views, not only in a blueprint for change, but also in the very fabric of activities that will bring that change about.

We would like to single out and thank those who presented their critiques of the MBA phenomenon and ideas for change and reconstruction at the Future of the MBA conference: Henry Mintzberg (McGill University), Jeffrey Pfeffer (Stanford University), James O'Toole (University of Southern California), and their discussants: Dean Dipak Jain (Northwestern University, Kellogg School of Management), Dean Alison Davis-Blake (University of Minnesota, Carlson School of Management), Dean Jordi Canals (IESE), and Dean Joel Podolny (Yale School of Management). We would also like to acknowledge our debt to the late Sumantra Ghoshal's epistemologically informed critique of the intellectual and sociological landscape of business academia. We would like to thank our panel of academic presenters: Ron Burt (University of Chicago), Bill McKelvey (Anderson School of Management, University of California at Los Angeles), Chris Argyris (Harvard University and Monitor, Inc.), and Michael Jensen (Harvard University and Monitor, Inc.), and their discussant, Sarah Cliffe, Executive Editor of the *Harvard Business Review*. Special thanks to the Hon. John Ralston Saul for his incisive and insightful presentation on the role of managers on the social, economic, and cultural landscape of the twentieth century.

We would like to thank everyone who joined us in Toronto for their presence of mind and body and the application of their psychic energies to the high-caliber dialogue that characterized the conference from beginning to end: Robert Bauer, Brendan Calder, Melanie Carr, K. C. Chan, Joseph D'Cruz, David Dunne, Lawrence Feick, Jim Fisher, Heather Fraser, George Gau, William Glick, Ned Hill, Santiago Iniguez, Xavier Mendoza, Ajay Patel, Peter Pauly, Paul Portney, Lawrence Pulley, Myron Roomkin, Joe Rotman, David Samuel, John Seybolt, Dilip Soman, Julia Tyler, and Glen Whyte. Without the deans who joined us in Toronto, the dialogue would have necessarily remained toothless. Without Steve Arenburg of the Rotman School, who expertly helped to organize and discipline us all, the conference would have remained at the level of a plan or blueprint.

Finally, a word about those to whom this book is dedicated: Joe Rotman and Marcel Desautels, through their visionary gifts and encouragement over the past ten years, have made possible that which remains all too rare in our world today—the pursuit of intellectual entrepreneurship of the kind that turns ideas into behavior. For this, they have our enduring gratitude.

Contents

Figures

The Future of the MBA

Introduction

The Future of the MBA and the MBA of the Future

We see others not as they are, but as we are.
The Talmud

The Master of Business Administration (MBA) degree is a currently successful North American-originated cultural artifact and socioeconomic phenomenon that has gained worldwide acceptance, consisting of a two-year educational experience in which college-trained students with typically two to four years of work experience get the opportunity—on passing through a selective filtering process—to "train for managing a business." Demand for the MBA degree currently exceeds supply by a healthy margin, and the top "producers" of MBA trainees are large, profitable, and growing enterprises. However, a number of vehement critiques of the MBA degree have emerged. They raise questions about its economic, intellectual, practical, moral, and "all-things-considered" value and about its relevance and viability that translate into questions about its near and long-term future. These critiques—which we review and discuss here—are pursued along different lines and on different grounds, but they share a focus on the "future of the MBA"—about which they are pessimistic on the basis of their evaluation of various current trends.

Discourse about the "future of X" is, of course, predicated on the assumption that X—or some essential set of characteristics of it—will endure, such that X-in-the-future will still be recognizable as a continuation of X-now. There is, however, no reason to assume that the future-of-the-MBA will result in the MBA-of-the-future—it may, for instance, end up in extinction. Therein lies a dilemma the critiques jointly face: because they criticize the MBA phenomenon vis-à-vis a set of goals and objectives that are presupposed by the current institutional, economic, and intellectual

3

framework in which the current MBA phenomenon lives, they cannot simultaneously criticize the MBA *and* the very presuppositions in which the phenomenon is grounded and thus do not enable us to consider an MBA-of-the-future that may be radically different from the MBA-of-the-present. The task of revaluation of core values that must precede *de novo* design work, therefore, still lies ahead. It represents an unaddressed challenge. We argue that the "problem of the MBA" must be posed in new terms in order to register real progress on the current version of the MBA; that the problems of the future manager and organization will be different from the problems that the current MBA graduate and his or her training addresses; and therefore that conceptualizing the manager of the future must precede the design of the MBA of the future.

The "Competitiveness Critique": Is the MBA a Competitive Source of Human Capital for the Organizations of the Future?

Pfeffer and Fong (2002) question the value of the MBA to its graduates and position the "U.S.-style MBA" as an educational product endangered by competitive offerings. They argue that the MBA does not yield the advertised results (career advantages for graduates over non-MBA graduates); that higher achievement in the MBA does not lead to better job and career prospects; that the effective knowledge transfer that occurs during an MBA program can be and usually is replicated by short programs of "business acculturation" that consulting firms and investment banks run, in-house, for their freshly minted MBA hires, programs that bring the latter up to speed on the "business jargon" that functions as an effective internal communication code and barrier of entry to their chosen fields; and therefore that the MBA does not offset for graduates its sunk and opportunity costs. Their analysis rests on much anecdotal evidence—for instance, from MBA instructors' informal survey-based studies—but the evidence is convincingly marshaled, and it impressively aligns to support their claims.

The implication of their argument is clear: if the MBA has limited value as a developmental program, if the skills and knowledge that it imparts are of little value to its graduates, then an efficient labor market will seize on the gap between the value the MBA "industry" appropriates and the value that it creates for its graduates and employers and will implement a suitable correction. That this correction has not already been implemented by the market for managerial talent is due to market inefficiencies based on systematic but corrigible forms of irrationality that will be corrected, leaving the late-twentieth-century MBA as another in a series of speculative bubbles fueled by unjustified expectations and burst by the systematic testing and refutation of these expectations.

Pfeffer and Fong's analysis received significant attention in the business press. The responses focused squarely on the economic value of the MBA (see, for instance, Merritt, 2003) to show that getting an MBA is a positive-net-present-value course of action for putative graduates of leading MBA programs: "the MBA pays," these rebuttals argue, based on systematic data-driven studies. Of course, these answers do not address the *other* question raised by the Pfeffer and Fong analysis, which is: *Why* does the MBA pay? And, relatedly, *why* should the fact that the MBA pays *now* provide adequate grounds for us to believe that the MBA will pay in the future? After all, the decision to pursue an MBA will *always* be a future-expectations-sensitive decision, as the MBA trainee puts his or her career "on hold" for the two years required to complete the MBA program.

Some progress on this question can be made by focusing on the MBA as a selection mechanism rather than as a development program (figure I.1). In this sketch, the MBA program is part of a series of *selection processes* that begins during the years of elementary and secondary schooling and that includes college admissions processes, university grades and recommendations, work assignments, GMAT scores, and grades in graduate school classes. The MBA *qua* selection mechanism provides would-be employers with information about the *quality* of its graduates, in the form of easily interpretable grades and grade distributions and a degree from

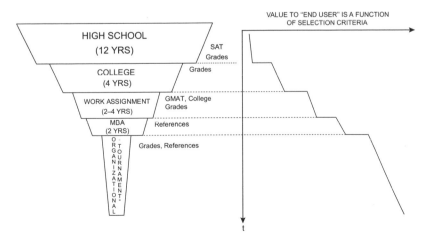

Figure I.I. A Deflationary View of the MBA Industry: The Selection Engine Argument

a school with a known set of selection criteria (i.e., a minimum entry standard and maximum admissions rate).

What characteristic is selected for in this process? is not a simple question to answer for many reasons, but, because this is a sketch, we pick two variables that are both significantly correlated to career success and plausibly *selected for* by the successive elimination process: general intelligence (g) (correlates to the tune of about 0.4 with 15-year job performance) and conscientiousness (C) (correlates 0.3 with 15-year-horizon job performance; see, for instance, Higgins, Peterson, Pihl, & Lee, 2006; Schmidt & Hunter, 1998). These correlations seem low, but, when understood as "compound rates of return" on personal capital, they become highly significant. There are good reasons to assume that the successive selection processes do pick out these two characteristics: standardized testing (GMAT) is weighted toward selecting for working memory and speed of associative processing of information (both correlated with g and together almost exhaustive of the variance in g), and grades are well correlated with conscientiousness when controlling for g (Higgins et al., 2006).

Whatever the value of such a filtering process to the "end-user" market, we can stipulate it as a lower bound on "the value of the MBA"—one that can be achieved regardless of the "skill boost" or the "content boost" that the MBA provides. Let us call this lower bound the "selection value" of the MBA. If the "selection value" of the MBA is high enough, then many, if not most, MBA-level "academic subjects" can be deleted from the training process (to achieve the efficiency gains of letting go of expensive faculty members) and replaced with any work that requires conscientiousness and g-related skills. This argument seems consistent with the existence of programs for retraining MBA's after business school (Pfeffer & Fong, 2002) that have taken shape in large consulting firms—a fact that is used to buttress pessimistic views of the *development* value of the MBA: if the conceptual knowledge base of the current MBA were useful to employers, there would be no need for "retraining," but only, perhaps, for *additional* training. On the other hand, if the MBA *certification* itself had no value, then these employers would not pay the price premiums associated with the MBA degree and would recruit elsewhere. Because admission to and graduation from the MBA program are prerequisites to certification, it is reasonable to posit that the value of the MBA is related to the selection function of these processes.

The implications of this argument are clear: if selection value dominates development value, then content does not matter as much as *process* does. Any system of training that (1) gets many more individuals to apply than can be accepted and thus has a credible threat of undersupply, (2) admits students on the basis of measurable individual characteristics that are plausibly correlated with after-graduation job performance, (3) gets them to engage in regulated, output-based competition on a series of tasks in which performance is correlated with general intelligence, conscientiousness, or both together, and (4) gets them to accept the resulting performance criteria and results as "fair" or "justified" succeeds in implementing a selection mechanism that is valuable to the market. If we additionally consider the "networking value" of the MBA degree (i.e., the resulting social capital of the graduates—facilitated perhaps by acculturation into a common "language of business" [Astley & Zammutto, 1992]) for the graduates, we will have achieved a sketch of an answer to the question that Pfeffer and Fong asked and that their critics never answered: Why *does* one pay—or pay as much as one now does—for an MBA?

Of course, the MBA "disciplines" are left in a difficult place by this analysis. If the MBA has no development value but only selection value, then the disciplines of the MBA have at best merely a symbolic value: they serve to *legitimate* the demands that the MBA places on its graduates. One could, for instance, ask would-be graduates to learn how to solve partial differential equations in a content-free fashion—without telling them what the variable names stand for—or to perform literary analyses of classic texts that develop important hermeneutic and analytical skills and then test proficiency to achieve a rank ordering of graduates that could be highly informative to prospective employers. This will suffice to fulfill the function of the MBA as a selection mechanism, but it will seem "irrelevant" to graduates and cause them to seek meaning in programs of study that purport to talk about "business" or about the "phenomena of business." Thus there is an important "make-believe" aspect to business education in the context of the MBA that—even if the "selection theory of MBA value" in its starkest form holds—educators must fulfill. However, in this selection model of the MBA, development is not a *source* of value—it is *epi*phenomenal relative to the success of the graduate.

Two sets of questions immediately arise: First, even if we accept the selection model, do we have the right selection criteria? Have we done as well as we could have in putting together the selection mechanisms of today? Do we have selection criteria that will correlate with future job and career success and organizational performance? We argue to the contrary and show that the high-value decision maker of the future will embody personal characteristics that go beyond algorithmic intelligence and conscientiousness.

Second, is development "dead" as a goal of the MBA? Is it the case that the most one can hope for in a two-year program of study is the reliable implementation of a selection mechanism that provides enough information to "end users" to discriminate among the "products"? We argue to the contrary again but show that the development aims of the MBA must be reconceptualized in the context of the "hermeneutic revolution" currently taking place in the environment that has been set up by the Information Age, which will require cognitive and behavioral skills and proclivities that *can* be seeded and nurtured in a program of intensive study—for which the MBA currently serves as a good placeholder.

The "Radical Structural Flaw Critique": Can the MBA Train Managers?

Mintzberg (2004) makes a radical argument that builds on the "MBA as selection engine" idea in a different direction. He argues that there is a "will to manage" and a set of often tacit capabilities essential to the craft and art of managing that constitute essential characteristics of would-be managers. These characteristics can be nurtured and developed but not explicitly inculcated and trained. They are not selected for by the selection procedures used to admit entering MBA students into master's-level programs of study, procedures that select for general intelligence and conscientiousness but not for the *je ne sais quoi* of the successful manager.

Moreover, because of the ineffable nature of these managerial skills (such as "the will to manage"—the successful art of taking and sharing responsibility), the MBA curriculum as it now stands, which relies on the classroom-based dissemination of explicit and cognitive knowledge structures and "business information," is in a poor position to either "teach" these skills or to cultivate them.

Indeed, if Mintzberg's argument is correct and the essential managerial skills can scarcely be articulated, the MBA enterprise is in a difficult position from the beginning, because it privileges cognitive knowledge over experiential knowledge and because explicit articulation is a precondition for the creation and validation of cognitive knowledge. Accordingly, he argues that the "design mind-set" that has been touted by no less of a paradigmatic exponent of the "cognitive revolution" than Herbert Simon can scarcely flourish in the environment that Simon and his intellectual descendants—such as Richard Cyert and Jim March—have contributed to creating in business schools, an environment that privileges—and cannot but privilege—theoretical *know-what* over and to the detriment of practical *know-how*. Thus MBA faculty members who are taken with Simon's call for a "design discipline" (Simon, 1986) are engaged in a collective illusion based on a performative contradiction: their activity sets and ways of being are not consistent with their espoused theories.

Consistent with his pessimism about the possibilities of the current MBA enterprise to implement a valid selection and self-selection system that picks out for development and promotion the possessors of the ineffable but essential skills of management, Mintzberg (2004) proposes a redesign of the selection process itself (see figure I.2), whereby, instead of the MBA program functioning as a selection mechanism for organizations, organizations function as a selection mechanism for the "professional MBA," which becomes a development program for senior managers. Candidates are selected into the "new MBA" on the basis of recommendations from their parent organizations, which in turn are based on *demonstrated*, rather than merely inferred, potential for managing. The "new MBA" is therefore a program in which the relative values of selection and development are reversed relative to the current MBA. Instructors are freed to design interventions that attempt to realize the development value of the MBA because the selection problem has already been taken care of by the market for talent. Thus, rather than contributing a selection filter to the market for talent, the new MBA takes advantage of the market for talent. What is gained, in Mintzberg's view, is a worthwhile "substrate" on which one can begin to work: managers whose promise has been validated by years of successful experience in dominance hierarchies—on which development-oriented interventions can flourish.

What is lost? First, the full selection value of the traditional MBA. If, as we have argued, there is a potentially large value that organizations attach to the selection function of the MBA, then this value evaporates once the selection function is contracted out to the employers by dismantling the current MBA enterprise. This value may be large

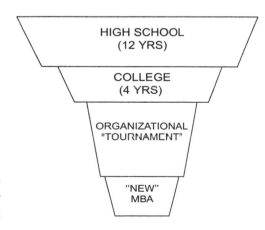

Figure I.2. Alternative "Selection Engine" View of Education

even if the selection criteria are imperfect, as the persistence of market enthusiasm for the MBA in the face of studies that have demonstrated the low impact of business academia on business practice (as Porter & McKibbin, 1988, have shown—with the notable exceptions of the impact of finance theory and financial engineering). Thus it is arguable that the elimination of the selection mechanism that the current MBA provides in favor of a model that transfers the selection function to the very private sector that now benefits from it is a not a strictly value-positive proposition. This argument, of course, does not vitiate Mintzberg's argument about the need for and propitiousness of a mid-career development program that nurtures nascent managerial skills; it simply challenges the premise that such a program can replace the MBA in an efficient fashion.

Second, the MBA concept that Mintzberg proposes can aptly be called a "tacit MBA." It is strictly a "taker"—not a "maker" or "shaper"—of managerial virtues, which are, in this case, whatever the participant's organization selects for. Thus, alongside subcontracting the selection task to the private sector, the "tacit MBA" also relinquishes the important task of *articulation* of the managerial virtues and of the problems of management to the managers themselves. It divests the function of *designing* managerial languages that will enable the managers of the future to pose and tackle problems that are not currently articulable. It does so because it rests on the premise that the essential skills of management cannot be made explicit; they are implicitly identified, must be implicitly trained, and can only be implicitly measured, via the proclivity of sponsoring organizations to send their managers back to the "tacit MBA" year after year (Mintzberg, 2006).

Without deemphasizing the importance of the tacit dimension that Mintzberg uses to ground his argument—indeed, we highlight its importance in our own reconstructive argument in chapter 1—the divestment of the *managerial design function* carries with it an unbalanced opportunity cost, for, with few and notable exceptions (see, for instance, Barnard, 1938; Sloan, 1965; and Grove, 2001), management practitioners are not usually competent *articulators* of their own competencies and thus are not good agents for the vicarious learning project that the MBA is, socially and culturally, part of. Concepts and theories are fallible, their use is often counterproductive, their importance is nefariously overplayed by current business academics to the detriment of implicit and hard-to-articulate skills, and their mindless deployment can stultify individual and organizational development; but, as Kurt Lewin put it, "there is nothing so practical as a good idea." Few things, indeed, are so valuable as a cognitive schema that guides the attention of the right person to the right variable or phenomenon at the right time and encapsulates, in a compressed and transmissible form, the experiences of many for the benefit of the recipient. To the extent that it promulgates the tacit dimensions of management to the detriment of the world of rigorous theorizing about managers and management, the "tacit MBA" undercuts the very important function that cognitive knowledge currently plays in the landscape of business organizations.

It is possible, however—as we show—to preserve the essence of Mintzberg's critique of current MBA programs and yet avoid both the unbalanced loss of the selection function they perform and that of their role as "knowledge agents." Doing so, however, will require a reconceptualization of "what knowledge is for," of what current business academics do and could do, and an understanding of the full selection value that can be appropriated by MBA programs in their current form. Selection, we argue, once legitimated as a goal and consciously pursued, can be a steady source of value for business schools operating on the current educational model. The processes that lead to the creation and validation of cognitive knowledge, we also argue, can in themselves represent transferable cognitive-behavioral modules that function as valuable managerial tools. The "tacit dimension" remains alive and important as a space in which management education occurs, but the ongoing process by which cognitive knowledge is created and validated becomes an ongoing source of value.

The "Ivory Tower" Critique: Is the MBA Relevant?

Bennis and O'Toole (2004) focus their critique of the MBA on the structure of the "MBA complex," made up of social science-trained academics who have a quasi monopoly on teaching and research positions in business schools and who proliferate an approach to MBA education based on the systematic application of the scientific method to what they perceive to be the "problems of business." The scientific method, as practiced by business academics, consists in the articulation of hypotheses about managers, organizations, and markets and in the testing of these hypotheses against data sets that are representative of the phenomena to which these hypotheses apply.

Notwithstanding the usual and often pertinent questions regarding the intellectual honesty of the enterprise—in particular regarding the difference between the "espoused theory of knowledge" of business academics and their "theory-in-use," to use the language introduced by Chris Argyris (see Argyris, 1993a)—there is still a question, which

Bennis and O'Toole raise and pursue, regarding the usefulness of making this method the exclusive "entry standard" to the halls of business academia. The authors argue that the fact that academia refuses entry to those who do not apply themselves to creating knowledge through the use of the hypothetico-deductive method—by denying tenure to academics who do not publish in peer-reviewed "top tier" journals— results in the isolation of business academics from the "real problems" of business managers and in a counterproductive schism between relevance and validity (for which reliability usually functions as a proxy in the academic review process). Insisting on a unique definition of knowledge as the result of replicable studies that are unambiguously interpretable in the context of theories of individuals and organizations often means that the "real problems" of practitioners of business are ignored. Barring practitioners and academics who are successful in the classroom or who publish in "practitioner journals" (such as the *Harvard Business Review* and the *California Management Review*) but do not also publish in peer-reviewed journals from tenured teaching and research positions in business schools amounts to the creation of a monopoly on the dissemination of business knowledge made up of individuals whose knowledge is divorced from practical application and whose ideas are often irrelevant to practitioners.

Bennis and O'Toole look for inspiration for changes in the "MBA complex" to law schools and medical schools, which—in their view— have created a happy synthesis between research, teaching, and practice. Academic medicine is set up to allow researchers and teachers to also carry on productive clinical practices that inform their research with practitioner-relevant problem statements and their teaching with practice-based examples and stories. Academic law is set up to allow law professors to carry on legal practice in either private or government posts, and it is this practice that informs the theoretical arguments that they put forth in their scholarly work. Bennis and O'Toole call for changes to the institutional rules that govern business academia, changes that are meant to allow practitioners and practice-oriented academics to teach in business schools and to enjoy decision rights similar to those of their colleagues who are now tenured on the basis of "pure" academic achievement alone.

Their prescription for change must rest, however, on a favorable view of the success of the law schools and medical schools in training competent practitioners of law and medicine, and herein lies a large potential problem: there is a significant difference between managers on the one hand and physicians and lawyers on the other, namely, the fact that, whereas graduates without MBAs can be managers, a graduate without a JD or an MD cannot be a lawyer or a physician, respectively. "Officially" trained lawyers and physicians have a monopoly over key areas of practice in their fields: arguing cases before courts and producing and documenting binding agreements, in the case of lawyers, and legitimately deploying the technologies for investigating and (surgically or pharmacologically) treating illness, in the case of physicians. Non-MBAs, by contrast, are not legally enjoined from managing organizations, and many paradigmatic cases of business success come from precisely the ranks of entrepreneurs who do not have MBAs. Therefore, there is no "market test" for legal and medical services that can be used to discriminate between legitimate JD-trained lawyers and legitimate but non-JD-trained lawyers or between legitimate MD-trained physicians and legitimate but non-MD-trained physicians in the same way in which the "market for managerial talent" can be used to adjudicate the relative merits of an MBA. Thus there is no way to perform the important experiment of gauging the relative market value of an MD to a physician, because there is no (legitimate) non-MD physician to supply the "control" case. If an MD degree actually *hindered* the human and professional development necessary for the creation of "better healers," we would never know it. This objection hurts Bennis and O'Toole's argument to the extent that it relies on pointing to academic law and medicine as "success stories" in virtue of the structural properties of their respective academic complexes. The current MBA, by contrast, appears to be itself a success story because it has withstood very difficult market tests and because the "MBA complex" has itself prospered as a result of this growth.

On the other hand, one can interpret their argument as pointing to academic law and medicine as examples of cohabitation and integration between research and practice, examples that MBA programs could emulate in order to escape the irrelevance trap that the current "ivory tower" elite is in (Bennis & O'Toole, 2004). The argument for change is weaker in this interpretation because it does not rely on a persuasive reason for foregoing academic rigor in favor of greater relevance to practitioners, but it is still worth exploring. It is also open to a powerful counterexample, which the authors do not consider. Engineering schools *do* face similar "industry conditions" to those in which the MBA complex operates (no monopoly position of practitioners is sustained by the regulatory environment, so one can practice engineering design without accreditation from an approved engineering school). They are successful as consistent and acknowledged sources of graduates who are both engineering practitioners and high-technology entrepreneurs. Yet the profession rests on an inner core of tenured academics who are often not practitioners and who do *not* write in practitioner-oriented journals. Indeed, the *IEEE Transactions* series (*Communications, Information Theory, Signal Processing, Circuits and Systems, Geoscience and Remote Sensing, Microwave Theory and Techniques, Systems, Man and Cybernetics* and *Wireless Communications,* to name but a few examples) effectively functions as a "gold standard" for tenure review processes, yet many of the papers published therein have only tenuous connections with the world of "engineering practice."

The academic version of engineering design problems is often based on assumptions that—for the sake of analytical tractability and logical auditability—do not correspond to the design conditions faced by engineers "in the real world." The "hot problems" of academic engineering disciplines are often not the "hot problems" of engineering practice. In spite of the analytical cult of the academic engineering disciplines, however, the engineering educational complex as a whole is successful because of the intimate kinship between the cognitive and behavioral skills required to solve an academic engineering problem and those required to solve a problem of "engineering practice."

As we show later, the success of such programs rests in the transfer of valuable "know-how" in conjunction with the theoretical and factual "know-what." Educational success in a competitive environment is not tied to the successful inclusion of "practitioners" into the academic "power core," nor to the inclusion of "practical problems" into the "acknowledged problem base" of the academic discipline—essentially the moves proposed by Bennis and O'Toole for the MBA complex—but rather to a happy confluence between the types of skills required to solve the "problems of academic engineering" and the "problems of applied engineering." Given that there exists a space in which valuable practical skills are isomorphic to valuable academic skills—and we show this to be the case for business disciplines as well—the transfer of the valuable "academic artifact production" (arguments, papers, and books) skills will also lead to the transfer of valuable practical skills.

Should our argument prove to be correct, it would also address the most glaring fault of the Bennis and O'Toole thesis, which relates to its implementation: why, in the absence of immediate market-driven incentives (which are currently lacking), should the academic, tenured power core of business academia want to change the makeup of their discipline and give significant decision rights to individuals who are not likely to speak the academic language in which agreements are reached or forged? Why should individuals who often intrinsically value precision and analytical rigor and closure (subject to a minimum-wage requirement) make the trade-offs between internal coherence and external validity that would be required to accommodate practitioners who speak their minds in the form of anecdotes, hunches, riddles, and difficulties, rather than assumptions, hypotheses, initial and boundary conditions, and critical tests? In virtue of what should the resulting coordination and political costs be incurred by the current MBA complex?

Granted, the Bennis and O'Toole argument is addressed to business school *deans*, but what arguments do the said deans have to buttress *their* demands—provided they take the argument to heart—for change addressed to their senior faculty members? Addressing these problems—even if we recognize the relevance gap as a problem of business academia—requires a reconceptualization of the role of business academia and of the role of academic knowledge *of* business *to* business. We develop such a reconceptualization and present ways in which the current MBA complex can remain close to relevance and build value from its core for future practitioners.

The "Deprofessionalization" Critique: Is the MBA a Viable Institution? Is Management a Viable Profession?

Pfeffer and Fong (2004) respond to studies (incited by their 2002 critique) purporting to show that the MBA is a positive-financial-value proposition by decrying the focus on these exculpations on cash value alone. Presenting the MBA—as many schools do—as a way to make more money more quickly has negative long-run effects on the professionalism of trainees, on the motivations and (through self-selection) the personal characteristics of entering students, and on the motivations and activities of faculty members. Placing MBA schools in competition with one another and making the financial return to graduates a significant component of the ranking metrics creates dynamics that undermine the professionalism of the field as a whole and creates adverse incentives stemming from well-known hidden information and hidden action problems. Pfeffer and Fong attempt to establish a link between the instrumentalist mind-set of MBA schools and their graduates and the proliferation of "ethical disasters" that have shaken investor confidence in public corporations and public confidence in the ethics of managers in recent years.

The proliferation of exclusively pecuniary incentives in business leads to the erosion of trust in the management profession as a whole and, simultaneously, to the dissolution of the professional core of the MBA academic complex. Entering students who value cash and career success above other potential rewards that organizational life and work can bring them select themselves into the applicant pool—and schools' own marketing and promotional materials, which stress money and success as tangible rewards of the MBA, fuel this self-selection process. Competition for grades within the schools, coupled with the instrumentalist ethos of the students, drives down the quality of the educational process and promulgates substandard ethical behavior aimed at getting a better grade without regard to deservedness or the cultivation of the underlying qualities that the grade is supposed to proxy for. Emphasis on student satisfaction as a key metric of a school's performance—which is particularly important in the competition among business schools—serves to make student satisfaction a key metric for the evaluation of instructors, which leads in many cases to the diminution of standards of academic quality and teaching effectiveness and the proliferation of the "entertaining dissemination of information"—or "infotainment"—in the MBA classroom. The resulting spiral is self-fueling: higher payoffs lead to the self-selection of more ruthless pursuers of wealth and success into MBA programs, which in turn leads to greater competition among graduates and schools and lower standards of ethics, intellectual honesty, achievement, and cooperation. Thus deprofessionalization is an accelerating phenomenon, and the response of the business press to the authors' original critique of MBA programs serves to exemplify and emphasize the trends and tendencies that accelerate it.

Although it is not clear that its authors had envisioned this, the deprofessionalization critique of the MBA touches on both the selection value and the development value of the degree. Whereas lower standards of integrity and intellectual honesty affect the development value of the MBA, lower standards of academic performance and grade inflation and the proliferation of infotainment as a preferred mode of interaction between instructors and students decreases the informational value of grades and academic achievement in the MBA classroom to prospective employers, as does the increased prevalence of cheating in the MBA classroom, coupled with the decreased proclivity of MBA schools to punish cheating when it is discovered (Pfeffer, 2006). One is left with the value of the MBA admissions process only as an effective selection mechanism that rests on *admission standards,* not on relative performance, a mechanism that inseparably couples the benefits of intelligence- and conscientiousness-based selection with the expected costs of the self-selection of increasingly instrumental and ruthless entrants into the MBA program. Of course, the market for managerial talent could be signaling, by the positive value it attaches to the MBA degree, that guileful self-interest is itself one of the valuable attributes of graduating MBAs, rather than an expected cost of the selection mechanism embodied in the MBA.

Pfeffer and Fong's reconstructive argument suggests that one possible solution lies in a reprofessionalization of the field of business research and teaching through the standard instruments of institutional imprinting, which have worked well for academia for several hundred years. Business schools should come to understand themselves as university departments composed of scholars with a vested interest in the promulgation and development of learning skills that are valuable to graduates across the span of long organizational careers: "lifelong learning skills," to use the propagandistic vernacular. Because the value of these skills is not immediately measurable and part of a complex causal nexus in which the MBA experience is implicated, this conceptualization of the purpose of the MBA deemphasizes immediately measurable costs and payoffs of the MBA degree to the MBA graduates and to the MBA schools. Something akin to the intrinsic or long-run value of an MBA education must be taken into account by the potential applicant when making his or her decision to get an MBA, which, in turn, can serve to increase the rate at which students who recognize the intrinsic or long-run value of learning (as opposed to those who insist on immediately measurable pecuniary value) self-select themselves into the applicant pool.

The proposal suffers from the implementation difficulty that it relies on business schools' ability and willingness to collude to introduce institutionalization measures that in the short run can be deleterious to the competitive position of any one school or group of schools that introduce them. An understanding that business schools are conventional academic departments of large universities is also likely to be resisted by the academic departments themselves, which have benefited significantly from the profits brought in by what they consider to be their "less rigorous" counterparts.

However, even supposing that such difficulties can be surmounted, there is a challenge that Pfeffer and Fong's reprofessionalization prescription for the MBA must squarely face, which is that of articulating precisely what the "lifelong learning skills" that the MBA cultivates are and how MBA academia, in its current state, can cultivate these skills in MBA graduates. The challenge is a tall one, for, if we consider critiques such as the "ivory tower" argument of Bennis and O'Toole, the relevance gap between business research and business practice raises questions about the possibility that MBA programs can impart the kind of lifelong learning skills that are particularly relevant to business. We answer this challenge by showing the work of academics *qua* researchers to provide a logic of articulation, inquiry, and validation that *is* valuable to managers and whose value should be expected to grow in time. By making clear the connections between the logic of science and the logic of business, we will arrive at a characterization of the work of business academics that can function as a foundation for the lifelong learning experience that Pfeffer and Fong envision.

The "Vicious Hermeneutic Circle" Critique: Is the MBA "Good for Business and Society"?

For Ghoshal (2005), the MBA is fundamentally "bad for business"—and society—because it cultivates emotional landscapes, actional tendencies, and cognitive habits that are counterproductive. How? Through what Ghoshal terms a "double hermeneutic": scholars articulate, validate, and teach what they (sometimes even honestly) present as descriptive theories about humans, organizations, and society—theories that purport to show them *as they are*. However, these theories have embedded within them often-hidden assumptions that are not themselves ever tested (or even made explicit): about "human nature" and the representational tropes used to articulate salient features of it; feasible opportunity sets for production and exchange; the range of possibilities for structuring and destructuring human interactions; and so forth. However, because of the "scientism" of the breed of professionals that has taken over the "teaching of business," these assumptions are never brought out in open dialogue. Why not? Because such a dialogue would necessarily have to recognize the importance of ontological and metaphysical differences that have been "banished from science" by the "arch-scientists" of the early twentieth century—as they are not resolvable by appeals to intersubjectively agreeable evidence statements (or "data," as they are reverently called) alone. Allowing such a dialogue to take place would undermine the appearance of "scientificity" in the social sciences—an appearance that has been hard-won. Thus normative assumptions end up parading—misleadingly—as descriptive "truth."

A case in point, in Ghoshal's view, is that of agency theorists, who have started from the assumption that managers' interests are dominated by pecuniary concerns and are frequently in tension with those of the organization that employs them. They have come to understand organizations as contractual adaptations to a state of perpetual potential conflict of interest between managers and shareholders and have focused their empirical efforts on understanding the effects of aligning manager-shareholder incentives on the financial value of the organization. Thus they have crafted successful courses in finance and general management departments of business schools that teach—often implicitly and "undiscussibly"—a pessimistic underlying view of human nature in the guise of a useful set of empirically justified rules and heuristics for designing employment and exchange contracts.

Opening up what Ghoshal perceives to be fundamental assumptions of agency theory ("people want stuff, money buys stuff, therefore [!] people want money"; "people will trade a small enough quantity of any one good [say, integrity] for a large enough quantity of some other thing [say, sexual gratification]") to debate or criticism is problematic because it opens up arguments that cannot be settled by recognized "scientific means" alone (articulating hypotheses, specifying conditions under which these hypotheses would be found to be false, seeking data that signals the occurrence of these very conditions, and concluding in favor of the hypotheses only if such data cannot be found). It would also open up realms of moral disagreement that have metaphysical, epistemological, and ontological dimensions that current academic discourse is not broad enough to handle.

Thus a kind of determinism is set in place—in Ghoshal's model—with regard to the pessimistic assumptions of the theory: they become self-fulfilling because they are taught—implicitly—as injunctions rather than descriptions, even though they originally started out simply as unspoken assumptions that helped theorists come up with an analytically tractable conceptual tool that is amenable to empirical testing. Taught that "people want money"—the story goes—managers *end up* valuing money above other possible ends of their organizational relationships. Taught that (many) people are "self-interested, with guile"—as they are by those who teach organizational theory classes based on the transaction costs economic paradigm—managers end up *more likely themselves to be* purely "self interested, with guile." Of course, *this* is itself a testable hypothesis that (apparently unbeknownst to Ghoshal) *has been tested*: Frank, Gilovich, and Regan (1993) find that cooperative tendencies of graduate students, upon training in the (self-interest-based axiomatic foundation of) microeconomic analysis, decrease significantly relative to those of peers trained in other disciplines.

The self *can* be malleable and does offer potentially fertile grounds for Ghoshal's double hermeneutic to work. However, neither Ghoshal's indictment of "dominant management theories" nor his prescriptive conclusions follow from his analysis. First, agency theory (for instance) is conceptually flexible enough to accommodate broader and less pernicious assumptions about human behavior yet remain useful. Retain maximization-based *choice* as a fundamental interpretive device for understanding behavior (as opposed to "biological" or "social" causes or "cultural or social rules"); replace "money" with "value"—however conceived by the individual; refine the substitution principle to include singularities caused by nonfinite rates of substitution among goods (e.g., between integrity and money); and increase the scope of feasible owner-manager contracts to include the value-creation frontier normally excluded by distributive contracts, and one will have recreated an agency theory that can function as a useful tool for organizational design and managerial intervention (see Moldoveanu & Martin, 2001).

Because of the very "underdetermination of theory by evidence statements" (references to which date as far back as Duhem, 1913/1989) that Ghoshal (implicitly) uses to argue against the incontrovertibility of pernicious and prevalent current organizational theories, we are led to challenge his assertion that "the fault is in the theories." It is not: the theories can be repaired, improved, refined—changed, ultimately. A richer set of interactions among academics and between academics and the phenomena they study can *help* the process by which theories become more useful—and in this light, Ghoshal's call for a renewed *pluralism* in academic interactions makes sense. But it is not guaranteed to provide a *solution* to the problem he sets forth—the problem of the double hermeneutic. For *pluralism in itself* does not guarantee a broadening of the discursive boundaries of a discipline or of a communication community, which can easily "fall into" commonly accepted ontological and epistemological assumptions simply as convenient simplifications that allow a tricky institutional coordination game to unfold (see, e.g., Pfeffer, 1993; Moldoveanu, 2002, for two very different views of the same phenomenon). Nor is pluralism in business academia in itself called for by Ghoshal as the solution to a particular problem that confronts contemporary managers.

There is a "missing conceptual link" here, leading from Ghoshal's diagnosis to his suggested solution. Our analysis vindicates Ghoshal's intuition about the solution, even as we have shown his diagnosis to be too simplistically based on a theoretical determinism that is untenable in virtue of Ghoshal's own epistemological attitudes. We show that even though the double hermeneutic of "gloomy ideological visions turned into prescriptive science via scientistic self-misunderstanding" is *not* the main problem facing the MBA community, ontic and epistemological pluralisms *are* part of the solution.

Critiquing the "Future of the MBA" Requires Articulating a Vision for the "MBA of the Future"

Several ideas have come to the fore in this preliminary critique of the critics. First, it is helpful to recognize both the value of the MBA as a selection mechanism that performs a useful information processing function in the market for managerial talent—what we have called the MBA's *selection value*—and the value of MBA studies as a program of human development, materialized through the identification, development, and refinement of skills that are useful to the organizational decision makers of the near and the far future. Critiques that do not distinguish between these two sources of value risk imperiling their own validity and persuasive force. Even if it is the case, for instance, that the MBA *should ideally* offer significant development value to its graduates and their prospective employers, it can nevertheless remain valuable on the basis of its selection value alone: as we have shown, plausible selection criteria for entry to an MBA program (such as general intelligence and conscientiousness) *are* correlated with individual career performance to degrees that are high by the standards of the statistical validation of law-like statements in the social sciences. Critiques that do consider the selection function of the MBA but believe that it can be better performed by organizations and markets for talent than by business schools relying on the use of standardized testing and achievement records and that are simultaneously pessimistic about the development value of the MBA—such as Mintzberg's—must account for the high value that markets consistently place on MBA graduates, a value that must reflect the desirability of the selection mechanism the MBA implements at a precise time in the typical graduate's working life cycle. Of course, recognizing the selection value of the MBA as a significant influence in graduates' and employers' decision processes does not mean that this value cannot be increased by the redesign of the selection mechanisms. Indeed, it is not clear at all that MBA programs have self-consciously understood themselves as selection mechanisms and therefore as shapers of the characteristics of the managers of the future.

To our knowledge, no rigorous analysis has been applied to date to measuring the relationship between MBA selection metrics and long-run managerial and organizational performance. Rather, MBA programs have accepted the *status quo ante* of the technologies for selection and have gone along with the postsecondary educational complex as a whole in their choice of selection metrics, in a classic case of institutional imprinting that has gone unchallenged and unquestioned. In the meantime, psychometric technology has advanced to the point at which personality traits, prefrontal cortex function, perceptual acuity, open-mindedness, the effectiveness of executive functions such as the self-control of behavior and cognition, and interactions among all of these characteristics can be reliably measured and correlated with human performance. At the same time, the fundamental elements of managerial skills and intelligence have been analyzed and decomposed into canonical skill sets that in turn can be used to generate even more specific measures of managerial potential.

To date, however, these advances in the measurement of human performance have gone untapped by the MBA educational community— indeed, by *any* educational community.

In this case, are conscientiousness and general intelligence the best that we can do in terms of ranking metrics that then turn into selection criteria for the managers of future organizations? To answer such questions, we need a conception of the MBA of the future to complement our discussion of the future of the current MBA. It requires answers to the following questions: What problem are we trying to solve when we do what we do? What is the purpose of the selection processes embodied in the MBA of the future? What are the canonical characteristics that are likely to correlate with managerial success in the twenty-first century, and how are these characteristics related to what we can currently measure using the best available psychometric techniques? It is only relative to such a mission statement that the relative value of alternative or complementary measures of human capacity and performance can be judged; and the articulation of such a mission statement is one task that markets cannot carry out for us.

Answering such a question is no less important to articulating a blueprint for enhancing the development value of the MBA of the future than to articulating a plan for enhancing its selection value. As with selection mechanisms and the ranking metrics that define the fitness function for any individual applicant, it is important to *articulate* the skills and proclivities that the MBA of the future will aim to cultivate and refine and to show how precisely these skills and tendencies will add value to contemporary and future organizations. A view of the "high-value decision maker" of the future is required before a substantial critique and reconstruction project for the MBA can proceed. For this reason, we proceed, in chapter 1, by first articulating and arguing for a particular conception of the high-value decision maker of the future, embodying skills and characteristics that make him or her a different creature from the prototypes for managerial success on which current versions of the MBA curriculum and design philosophy rest. We show why this high-value decision maker of the future will be in great demand and short supply given current trends in educational and selection technologies and programs, and how the problems that that high-value decision maker must solve are a likely outcome of the current social and cultural context of business organizations. In chapter 2, we show why MBA academics and training programs do not address the problem of producing the desired high-value decision maker and trace the problem to the sociology of the basic disciplines of management science, the institutional and microincentive structure of business academia, and the epistemological orientations of business academics.

In chapter 3 we show that, contrary to expectations, business academia *can* assume leadership in training the high-value decision maker of the future with nondisruptive changes to its institutional structure. Indeed, we show that the development of high-value decision makers can profit significantly from the methods and skill sets of social scientists themselves, who, by teaching what they *do* rather than what they *know*, can significantly enhance the development value of the MBA of the future. Delivering on this potential will, however, require a reconceptualization of the nature of knowledge and learning and of the role of academics in the production of knowledge and the promulgation of learning.

The Integrative Thinker

A Vision of the High-Value Decision Maker in Postmodern High Capitalism

This is my way. What is your way? The way—that does not exist.
Friedrich Nietzsche, Also Sprach Zarathustra

One often thinks of labor markets—and of the market for managers in this particular case—as collectively embodying the arbiter of what a valuable MBA program consists of. The market for managerial talent—in this view—defines the value of an MBA degree. What, then, is the role of a monograph on the future of the MBA? Is the exercise we are about to undertake really useful? The answer turns on the difference between an *arbiter* and a *designer:* a monograph can apply itself to a task that markets for managerial talent cannot tackle—the task of *articulation,* of introducing the new categories and concepts that will be causally relevant and instrumentally useful to the management students and educators of the future.

Although markets are proficient at attaching values to well-defined possible outcomes, via salaries for managers trained in different programs and institutions; at ranking alternative paths for achieving these outcomes via independent rankings of MBA and other training programs incorporating program-specific "measures of value"; and even at producing accurate point predictions of particular events, such as the transition of a particular program from one tier to another, they cannot *produce* new concepts and categories that will make the trained manager of the future a high-value decision maker. Markets are *concept takers*, not *concept makers*. Given a set of concepts and ideas, a market can rank them according to their expected economic value. It is the intellectual entrepreneurs, the educational venture capitalists, the pedagogical visionaries who must "stick their necks out" and fulfill the function of articulating these concepts, and that is the task we are taking on. We begin with a brief excursus on the semantics of this chapter's title.

"Postmodern": Why "Post"?

It is not because we want to knock modernity and its varied cultural, intellectual, and technological offspring but rather because we want to highlight the recent and abruptly growing failure of absolute—or unquestionably accepted—norms of legitimation and justification of knowledge, desire, belief, and action. What Jean-Francois Lyotard (1979) conceptualized as the demise of the "master narratives"—such as Marxism, *laissez-faire* capitalism, positivistic science, Lockean liberalism, and the systemic and totalitarian philosophies of Hegelian and post-Hegelian philosophers—has given rise to a multitude of ways of thinking and patterns of behavior—indeed, "life-forms"—that can be equally legitimate or illegitimate, depending on their context and purpose. There exist, in contemporary organizations, *many* value systems, *many* ways of knowing, *many* ways of acting and relating—many ways of managing—and *many* ways of choosing among them. In the postmodern era, *self-evidence is dead:* no single way is evidently valid to everyone in virtue of its claims. Monoparadigmaticity is a cultural relic, even though its emotional landscapes continue to function in many organizations and institutions and though it is still alive and well in many niches of academia. Panic, inaction, malaise, *akrasia*—or weakness-of-the-will—and Durkheimian *anomie*—or ambivalence about core values and ways of living—are often the symptoms of the new pluralism, which now faces decision makers with hard choices that must be made on grounds whose legitimation derives from the very actions these choices engender, rather than from an accepted and legitimate set of reasons, values, principles, and methods. Legitimacy is *made,* not given.

To be successful on this new sociocultural landscape, the manager of the future must *act* in the face of the breakdown of certainty and self-evidence for the reasons of action; must *think* in the face of the looming paralysis induced by an awareness of the multiple ways of thinking available to him or her; must *experiment* and tabulate results in a disciplined fashion in the face of doubts about the incontrovertibility of "data" and the ultimate meaning of those data vis-à-vis a particular set of reasons for action; must *believe* in his or her grounds for acting in order to induce the right motivation to act in others; and must *act* in order to produce the right beliefs in him- or herself and others—all without falling into

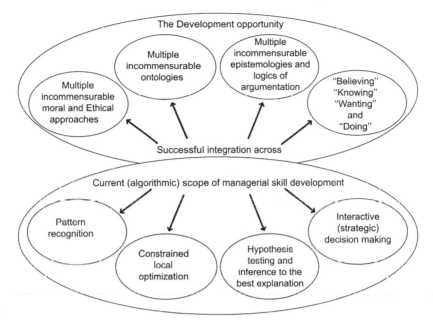

Figure 1.1. The Educational Opportunity in Postmodern High Capitalism

the epistemic and moral relativism that empties him or her of the vital trust that a better outcome is possible and achievable. He or she must be competent to internalize the *clash* among multiple, incommensurable views of the world and resolve this clash productively.

The postmodern condition of management may be understood as the percolation into organizational reality and managerial practice of dilemmas and conundrums that have inhabited the core of epistemology and analytical philosophy for several decades. Here are some of the most powerful results that we believe will shape managerial and organizational life in the near future:

Ontological Relativity

Quine (1951) posits and argues for the radical indeterminacy of translation from one way of representing the world in words to another. An organization is variously viewed by academics as a nexus of contracts among self-interested principals and agents (Jensen & Meckling, 1976); as a more or less mechanical production function that combines inputs in ways that permits it to claim revenues in excess of costs—as in the neoclassical economic model; as a network of relationships among human individuals (Burt, 1999) or among deterministically or probabilistically

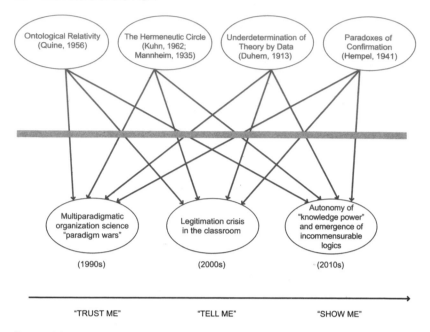

Figure 1.2. The Percolation and Diffusion of Legitimation Crises into Business Academia and Managerial Practice, 1990–2020 A.D.

coupled activity sets (McKelvey, 1999); as a set of power-based relationships (Pfeffer, 1978); or as a community of knowledge and learning (Argyris, 1993a; Moldoveanu, 2001)—among other possible theoretical lenses and metaphors. It can be viewed by managers as a machine, an organism, a brain, a mind, or a tribe (see, e.g., Morgan, 1997, for an explicit view of the role of powerful and popular metaphors in structuring pictures of organizations and of organizing).

What Quine's argument regarding the radical indeterminacy of translation indicates is that these different representations—which come alive through managerial action and make themselves into separate realities—cannot be guaranteed to connect to each other: How does a machine "talk" to a brain? How does it relate to a mind? A "nexus of contracts" language is not fully reducible to a "production function" language, nor, indeed, to an "activity set" language. "Natural selection engine" theories have no easily discernible conceptual space to accommodate "network" theories of organizing, and vice-versa.

What does this mean for managers who understand the problem—or who "live it," even without understanding it? It means that they must make choices that cannot rest on a sound logical argument: they must settle for a merely *valid* one. A sound logical argument is an argument from incontrovertibly valid premises through to incontrovertibly valid conclusions. By contrast, a merely valid inference does not guarantee the validity of its own premises, only the fact that the truth value of the premises are carried through to the conclusions: if the premises are false, the conclusions will also be false. "Soundness" must be earned or made. In choosing among different possible ways of conceptualizing their tasks, activities, roles, relationships and aims, a manager must make choices that are hard because no incontrovertible premises on which to build a justification for their choice exist. *This is my way*—says Nietzsche's Zarathustra; *what is yours? The way (...) does not exist.* The logic of *correctness* is—as it must be—superseded by the logic of *meliorism,* to use a Deweyan term: instead of aiming to make perfect or correct ontological or methodological choices, *better* managers make *better* ontological choices. Of course, in order even to begin to pose the challenge of meliorism, the very concept and problem of ontological choice must be understood and accepted before it can be cultivated as a core managerial capability.

The hermeneutic circle (and, only very rarely, *spiral*) of *theory→method→ observation→interpretation→new theory,* which was pointed out in the evolution of sciences (Kuhn, 1962) and social and political ideologies (Mannheim, 1935), highlights the extent to which ways of representing and investigating the world and ways of intervening in the world are coupled and connected together—into paradigms, in Kuhn's (1962) formulation, and into ideologies, in Mannheim's (1935) earlier formulation. What you know, how you know it, what you take to be real, and what you take the import of reality to be in the constitution of knowledge are intertwined. Choices of ontologies and epistemologies are interconnected, and, in turn, connected to the *practical* problems the knower takes him- or herself to be addressing. It is not usually possible to define selection criteria that apply equally well to two or more paradigms or ideologies, and therefore it is not possible to come up with a *trans*-paradigmatic quality metric of the quality of a theory. Each paradigm makes sense—or not— only within its *own* standards of epistemic rationality.

Postmodern management can be understood as the *design of successful action in a world of multiple competing paradigms that form self-fueling and self-sealing hermeneutic circles.* The typical tension or conflict between engineering and marketing departments, for example, is only superficially about the negotiation of acceptable feature sets and product delivery deadlines among individuals with differing interests and payoff sets that can be traded off against each other as part of the negotiation process. Even cursory examination of the discursive and communicative spaces and behavioral repertoires of individuals belonging to the two cultures reveals differences between commitments to the use of deductive, inductive, and abductive logics; differences in levels of reliance on anecdotal evidence and past personal experience as a way of grounding arguments about possible or desirable courses of action; differences between the operative ontologies of workspaces and organizations ('tasks," "projects," "theories," and "models" versus "relationships," "commitments," and "perceptions"); and differences in relative proclivity to engage in logically deep arguments based on narrow assumption sets as opposed to engaging in logically shallow arguments based on broad assumptions sets; among several others. Just as "nature, to be commanded, must be obeyed"—Francis Bacon's words— so radical difference, to be bridged and successful resolved, must first be understood, lest the resulting resolution or synthesis remain at the level of a negotiated outcome that is persuasive or meaningful to none of the transactants. What is required for successful managing in the world of parallel hermeneutic circles is a simultaneous engagement by the manager with *each* of these circles at the ontological, epistemological, logical, and pragmatic levels—and this, we argue, is the challenge that the new century poses to managers and educators everywhere.

The underdetermination of theory by observation statements (Duhem, 1913/1989) and the *underdetermination of observation statements by raw perceptions* (Anderson, 1978) make the selection of theories and models a matter of *choice* that is only *partially* based on data and the articulation of data a matter of choice that is at least partially based on (possibly unconscious) theories. Writing in 1913, Pierre Duhem articulated a thesis that took almost 40 years to register in the Anglo-American philosophical community—and it is still taking time to register in the American community of social scientists and business academics: briefly, that *data underdetermine theory,* in the sense that, even if a datum refutes a theory (by corresponding to a fact that has the opposite truth value from that of one of the logical consequents of the theory), it is still possible to salvage the theory by making changes to its assumptions, to the theories on which the measurement apparatus that has produced the datum is based, and so forth.

Suppose we as managers or organizational designers agree that we "want to maximize shareholder value": Should we divest our business unit operating in a profitable but nongrowing market to sharpen focus and get additional cash on the eve of an initial public offering (IPO)? Or, rather, should we keep and invest in the old business line to maximize overall revenues and—accordingly—the firm's chances of near-term profitability? There is one "theory" that argues that shareholders like "pure plays" in terms of products and markets and penalize firms that essentially take away their decision rights over the allocation of investment dollars to one market rather than another, a theory that receives some support from event studies in which divestitures of unrelated businesses are rewarded by markets with premiums over their previous, fully invested states. The theory also receives support from basic models of self-maximizing investor behavior, in which decision rights are valuable because they subsume the "option to change one's mind" and the "perception (illusory or not) of control," and, according to which, decision rights over market segment focus of capital investments should be given to investors rather than managers, who could misuse these rights by subsidizing unprofitable business units using cash from profitable ones to mitigate the overall risk of their organizations at the expense of an aggressive dividend policy that would be more closely aligned with the shareholders' own preference for risk.

So: divest? Closer examination of the event studies purporting to demonstrate a value premium associated with divestitures of unrelated businesses reveals that the divestitures in question were all in some way associated with an industry everyone fully expected to shrink dramatically (say, the U.S. defense industry during the era of the G. H. W. Bush and Clinton administrations), and thus the "data" could be explained equally well by a theory of "necessary consolidation," wherein the sellers reaped large positive benefits from both the consolidators and their own shareholders by (1) conducting efficient, value-maximizing auctions of their business units and (2) maintaining an aggressive dividend policy that allowed investors to capitalize on the outcomes of the auctions and gave them confidence to place and maintain cash in the hands of managers.

What about the "commonsense" theory that has investors valuing decision rights? What is the "evidence" for that? Well, a behaviorist might retort, how about the (so-called) "controllability bias," according to which individuals value control over actions that causally affect them—in the precise sense that they are willing to give something up in order to get or retain it. He or she might cite—as an example of the said "bias"—experiments in which the subjective experience of physical pain is substantially less aversive when the subject has some control over the infliction of the painful intervention than it is when the pain is inflicted by an external autonomous agent. Whether or not these data are indeed data for or against our commonsense theory of the value of capital allocation control to shareholders is not clear; for, in order to argue for the import of the "controllability bias" to the question about investor behavior post-IPO, one would have to also argue that these decision rights are either valuable in the hands of investors or potentially harmful to investors in the hands of managers, or both together. Suppose, to address the first point, that investors are uninformed and uninformable—because, for instance, they lack the cognitive skills and computational capacities to make the kind of market segment distinctions that managers can make—and they *know it;* is it unreasonable to assume that, *rationally,* they could prefer to place the relevant decision rights in the hands of managers and thus give them the reins to a carriage they know themselves to be incompetent to drive? Posing this question, of course, sets up yet another possible empirical test that has not yet been performed *but that is not essential;* what is essential is that no such test be immune from subsequent criticisms of the kind that we have raised, and therefore that the acceptance or rejection of an empirical test as relevant or dispositive of a theory will remain a matter of choice (see Lakatos, 1970, for an elaboration of this point).

John Anderson (1978) extended the Duhemian argument about the complex and nondeterministic relationships between theory and evidence, or data, by proving a theorem that asserts that the relationship between "raw experiences"—images in his case, although the argument can be extended to the other senses—and the "facts" that we usually take to correspond to these experiences is also not determined by the phenomenological properties of the experiences and the structural properties of language alone. In common language: What you say you see *does not depend only on what you see and the structure of English;* rather, there are, once again, *choices to be made* when you put experiences in words, even though these choices will often be influenced by *a priori* theories of which we may not always be conscious.

To the phenomenon of management, nothing could be more relevant than this seemingly esoteric result. For instance, a manager could ask of a predicament: "What are we experiencing now, in *this* discussion? A technical difficulty amenable to further analysis? A coordination problem caused by the fact that we use words in different ways? An *ennui* caused in one case by visceral factors (hunger, thirst, sexual arousal) and in others caused by the contagion of the original feeling of *ennui?* The manifestation of a latent conflict or tension caused by role overlap in the organization? A mismatch in moods, to be addressed simply by reconvening the meeting at some other time?" To each of these propositionalizations of the raw feelings involved there corresponds a possible *behavioral script,* such that choosing a particular propositionalization of the situation will—with some provisos and qualifications—usually lead to the enactment of a particular script: the "political conflict script," the "misunderstanding script," the "escalating mutual recrimination script," and so on. In turn, this means that the *wording* of the situation—the creation of text around it—represents at once a choice that is undetermined (by

Anderson's result) and very important, because it can trigger the enactment of scripts that in turn shape organizational outcomes.

Not surprisingly, therefore, we posit that the *articulator* role of the
manager—that of *talking the walk* and bringing to a shared and intelligi-
ble language the relevant raw experiences of the many—is among his or
her most important ones. It always has been, to be sure; what is different
about the postmodern epoch we have highlighted is that the articulation
function will rapidly become increasingly important, both because difference in and heterogeneity of worldviews are more manifest and also
because it will increasingly stand out against more mechanical or algorithmic skills and skill sets because of the decreasing marginal value of
the latter.

Paradoxes of confirmation (Hempel, 1941) complement *paradoxes of induction* (Goodman, 1974) and challenge the trust that one can reasonably
place in regularities as the building blocks of worldly knowledge. What
confirms—the question goes—a law-like statement such as "all ravens
are black"? A singular statement such as "here is a black raven," goes
the standard answer. However, there is a catch: because "all ravens are
black" is logically equivalent to "all nonblack objects are nonravens,"
therefore "all ravens are black" is also confirmed by "here is a pink
Jaguar"—that is, a nonblack (pink) nonraven (Jaguar). The link that goes
from evidence statement to hypothesis is not tight; it admits of equivoca-
tion and, accordingly, *choice.* The same argument carries through more
generally for inductive inferences. "Here is a blue emerald" confirms
the law-like statement "all emeralds are blue," but (Goodman, 1974) it
also—problematically—confirms the law-like statement "all emeralds
are bleen," by which a bleen object is blue on or before July 1, 2008, and
green on and after July 2, 2008. To the objection that "grue-bleen" language is "illegitimate" relative to "blue-green" language because it relies
on a time-dependent transformation of the respective predicates "blue"
and green," the "grue-bleen" user can reply that "blue-green" language
is illegitimate relative to "grue-bleen" language *for the very same reason:* for
an object that is green is *grue* on or before July 1, 2008, and *bleen* on or
after July 1, 2008. Once again, establishing the legitimacy of one of the
two language systems unambiguously to defenders of *both* language systems using *the same* argument is not possible: from within each of the two
language systems it is possible to consider the *other* one illegitimate without committing any logical fallacy.

How does the "grue-bleen/blue-green" dynamic play out in managerial life-worlds? Consider the all-important problem of interpersonal
trust between two protagonists. Does A behave trustworthily toward B
in order to gain B's trust to the end of deceiving B for profit at the right

time, or, rather, is A's behavior a valid proxy for a way of being that warrants B's trust? Just as "here is a green emerald" *simultaneously and equally* confirms *both* "all emeralds are green" and "all emeralds are blue," just so A's refusal to betray B *when he or she could have* can *simultaneously and equally* confirms "A is (genuinely) trustworthy" *and* "A is (instrumentally) attempting to gain B's trust for ulterior gain based on a timely breach of that trust."

The interactive cognition (sometimes superficially and euphemistically referred to as "mind games") pervasive in the business world is, of course, a happy hunting ground for such ambiguities of confirmation: Does the *other* duopolist make these quantity selections because he or she cannot figure out the Nash equilibrium of the duopoly game, because he or she does not "have the model right," because he or she has not focused on the same variables, or...? What is important here is not the (trivial) realization that managers "must act in the face of incomplete information and imperfect knowledge"—which almost always motivates a "sales pitch" for better information gathering and better information processing techniques or "skills"—but rather the point that "better managers act successfully in the face of *incompletable* information and *imperfectible* knowledge" by cutting through the Gordian knots that have always already been embedded in the foundations of the managerial "disciplines." The high-value decision maker of postmodernism is, we claim, an accomplished *experimental epistemologist,* independently of whether or not he or she conceptualizes his or her ways of being in these terms.

The Value-Ladenness of Theories

It is worth elaborating here on Ghoshal's critique of MBA education (Ghoshal, 2005): the theories that undergird both the "descriptive" social sciences and the "prescriptive" organization sciences have inside them an *undissociable* normative component that is often ignored because including it in academic, classroom, and boardroom discussions takes the discourse in these settings outside of the "scientific," "analytical," or "pragmatic" orientations that usually "feel comfortable" to the participants because it corresponds to their areas of training and expertise. However, comfort and validity are two different matters altogether: as Searle (2001) points out, even a seemingly "value-neutral" concept such as "truth" embeds a normative injunction or commitment, for the recognition of truth as a property entails a commitment to believe a proposition P if that proposition is true, or, at least, a preference for believing P given that P is true over not believing P given that P is true. To the convinced determinist, the ontological commitment of agency theorists to *choice* as a fundamental unit of human behavior (with the associated ontological "baggage" of responsibility, authority, and agency) will appear as a question-begging and value-driven one; just as the exclusive commitment of the deterministic social scientist to "causal chain" explanations of organizational behavior will seem an unwarranted one to the nondeterminist or the believer in free will.

The tension, then, between "goal setters" and "task designers," between "relationship builders" and "efficient transactors," between "symbolic actors" and "contract designers," between "idea-driven technological gurus" and "nothing-new-under-the-sun" and "everything-is-politics" believers must go beyond the kind of disagreement that can be resolved by the usual methods that academic science and "stylized reason" offer up. The value-ladenness of theories of behavior (and cognition) is an additional complication to the conundra we have discussed previously: for, if it turns out that choices among ontologies, epistemologies, representations, and methods must turn on extratheoretical considerations—especially on extratheoretical considerations that are likely to be "affectively hot" and relatively undiscussable or hard-to-discuss motivators of behavior—then what can we hope to teach the *ontological decision makers* of the future using the relatively benign interventions available to postsecondary educators (talking, writing, reasoning, arguing) and the affectively blunt toolkit of the academic (logic, analysis, the design of experiments and "studies")? The matter is even further complicated by the following condition.

The Undecidability of Problems of Choice among Values and Principles

Moral deliberation—deliberation about values and principles—is a different activity than the usual deliberation that forms the paradigm of classical rational choice, which is aimed at arriving at the optimal means to achieve a particular set of ends; it *deliberates about the ends themselves* and about the relative value of different ultimate ends. Is fairness to count more than efficiency as a measure of the outcomes of a team process? Should truth count for more than justice in a large-scale strategic decision-making process? Should the aesthetic value of the processes and procedures by which the means are chosen to match given ends be considered as an independent aim of the process of rational deliberation?

These are only on their faces abstract or theoretical questions; on the contrary, they are questions that have immediate and powerful implications for managers in their day-to-day activities. Should personal efficacy and efficiency count for more than horizontal equity in the design of compensation packages for senior executives? If they do, then individual incentives should be allocated without regard to fairness of the overall allocation to other team members. Should truth, or validity and accuracy, count for more than political expediency in a due-diligence process? If they do, then the marginal utility of additional information will dominate the marginal cost of additional units of deliberation or information foraging. Should aesthetic considerations—such as parsimony and elegance—be factored into the design of organizational rule systems alongside operational efficiency? If they do, does their admission as valid selection criteria for candidate rule systems enjoin managers from engaging in calculations aimed at measuring the marginal cost and benefit of a more "elegant" system of rules? Is it "aesthetically pleasing," in other words, to estimate the costs and benefits of aiming for aesthetically pleasing organizational solutions?

Rational-choice models—and much of the "theory" that is taught to would-be managers—are silent about these issues, as Ghoshal points out (2005), because they simply do not have the conceptual space to accommodate such deliberations. Attempts by analytical and moral philosophers to answer these questions—dating back to Immanuel Kant and running through the modern discourse ethics of Karl-Otto Apel and Jürgen Habermas—provide "solutions" that seem oblivious to the pragmatic constraints of modern organizational life. Kant's universalization principle, for instance ("act according to principles that would not be self-defeating if everyone else acted according to them") and Habermas's discursive universalization principle ("act according to principles that have been accepted by all interested parties through a process of ideal communication, or communication that is undistorted by power motives" [Habermas, 1993]) have great intuitive appeal as general maxims, but neither guarantees the existence of solution sets or the convergence of the process to a solution in a finite and predictable amount of time if a solution indeed exists—a constraint imposed on managerial action by the metronome of board meetings and quarterly earnings reports. Deliberation about values is, in general, *nonconvergent*. The value of the manager who is big-minded enough to understand the problem turns on what he or she makes of the phrase *in general*: the *engineering* of large-scale agreement on difficult issues involving differences of value *is* about the local solution of a problem that is *in general* not solvable.

The Nonconvergence of Reflective Deliberation

Nonconvergence problems are not limited to moral deliberation or to deliberation about values. They can also show up in rational deliberations, or deliberations about the best means for pursuing an agreed-on set of ends. *Given this situation, what to do?* is the question facing the manager every day. According to the rational-choice tradition, the first thing to do is to *think* about what to do and tabulate possible states of the world, payoffs associated with them, possible courses of action and probabilities for the various states of the world that are conditional on each of the possible actions, and calculate the expected value of the payoffs associated with each course of action. *Then what?* The standard rational-choice model says: act on the basis of a choice of the action that has the maximum expected payoff. This injunction glosses over the fact that the manager could choose to *think some more* and attempt to mitigate the uncertainty of the overall predicament through calculation or through further information gathering (see Lippman, 1991, for one possible formulation of the problem). So the *full option space* is not limited to the possibilities for *action* but also includes possibilities for *thinking further* and in different ways about the possibilities for action.

Are we now ready to write down the full decision model for the manager? No: *thinking about options and states of the world also has uncertain payoffs*. The manager can also choose to try to minimize *that* uncertainty by (that's right) *thinking about the possible ways to think* about his decision problem. But thinking about thinking also presents a set of uncertain payoffs—related to reductions in the uncertainty level associated with thinking, for instance. One can stipulate—as does Lippman—that thinking should stop when the uncertainty associated with another round of thinking is equal to the uncertainty associated with acting without thinking any further, or, as Moldoveanu (2005) suggests, when the marginal expected uncertainty reduction of the next round of thinking is offset by the marginal cost and uncertainty of the delay associated with the next round of thinking—but note that in either case we are talking about a feature of managerial thinking that is not part of the rational decision maker's standard repertoire, an *executive function* that monitors the structure, dynamics, and utility of *thinking itself* and *can control* the thinking processes involved in strategic deliberation.

We could say, at this point: "yet another potentially high-value skill not developed, selected for, or even identified in current MBA programs," but our criticism goes further and calls attention to the *nature* of the skill: it is extremely difficult to articulate, let alone teach, even though it seems clearly valuable to even basic decision-making processes in complex scenarios—and these difficulties are directly related to what is currently deemed teachable in the context of advanced educational programs, which is a set of functions and skills that can be *algorithmically represented,* or presented as a set of *recipes.* We argue later that what characterizes the contemporary organizational landscape is a *decrease in the marginal value of algorithmic skill sets,* relative to that of skill sets of the kind involved in the successful integration of parallel herme-neutic circles.

"High Capitalism": Whither "High"?

It is not because we want to extol the virtues of capitalism and highlight its triumph over other modes of organizing production and exchange but, rather, because the basic habits of the mind and behavior that character-ize progress in contemporary human dominance hierarchies—such as cost-benefit analysis as a decision-making technology, instrumental rea-son as a hermeneutic lens or logic for understanding oneself and others, the conceptualization of "the world" as a set of problems to be solved—have become widespread cultural artifacts, and the associated techniques for resolving "simple" and "complicated" problems in theory (via the computer and the algorithm) and in practice (via the successful outsourc-ing of increasingly complicated algorithmic tasks to efficient "optimiza-tion agents") have become *commoditized.* Informing, open-sourcing, and off-shoring (Friedman, 2005), combined together and with impressive-in-the-average productivity of low-cost manufacturing operations, have made it imperative to now take a fresh look at the "core" of manage-rial practice—that which is left over when all algorithmic activities have been efficiently subcontracted.

The Popularization of Dominant Logics of Explanation

What is remarkable about "high capitalism" is as much the increase in *both* the average and the marginal productivity of capital and labor as the entrenchment of certain logics that function as "explanation-generating-engines" for individual, organizational, and market behavior. Rational-choice theory and the logic of cost-benefit analysis have become requisite "communication technologies" for managers and many business scholars, even as they are being challenged in the academic disciplines in which they originated. Rational-belief theory and the explanation of belief formation using probabilistic logic—although used by a more restricted community of knowledge and communication—have become effective dominant logics of explanation for actuaries, investors, traders, and decision support system experts.

To understand the power of such logics, perform the following thought experiment. Try to articulate, to a strategic manager who is considering the effects of presenting and implementing a new compensation system design, a theory of employee behavior that is based either on *neurophysiological* processes alone—wherein employees are considered to be mere *organisms* that respond to microincentives that operate only on very short time horizons (minutes and seconds) and wherein responsiveness to either "reasons" or "long-term incentives" is an illusion that has been cultivated for reasons that can themselves be understood using the neurophysiological model—or on an ontology of mimetic desires (desires that mimic the desires of others) and culturally imprinted routines and habits alone—wherein human behavior is *pushed by causes* rather than *pulled by incentives,* which in turn renders the implementation of any forward-looking interest-based scheme at best a symbolic maneuver. The difficulty that you may have imagining how "the discussion would go" stems as much from the radical *ontological* differences between the three approaches to understanding human action as from the entrenchment of rational-choice language as a logic of explanation—from the difficulty of convincing an interlocutor who uses rational-choice logic that there exist such radically different alternatives that can also form viable "codes" for your conversation. Of course, the difficulty you may imagine is, we conjecture, a pale image of the difficulty you will *have* if you actually do try to carry out the "experiment" suggested by this paragraph.

The standard and dominant logic of explanation—based on the logic of expected-benefit-to-cost-ratio maximization coupled with a basic *technological* stance toward the world (Heidegger, 1973) which represents predicaments as a series of technical problems to be solved and objects and people as a set of means for addressing these problems—form the *cultural core* of high capitalism, which can be conceptualized as a shared cognitive engine that facilitates the design of efficient social and technical arrangements for the organization of work and exchange. So, then, does "high capitalism" come to dominate "postmodern capitalism"; that is, does the pervasive entrenchment of the "memes" associated with rational-choice theory, strategic planning, and algorithmic optimization in fact *force* a resolution of the deep problems that we have signaled to be at the core of any single explanatory logic?

We would argue it does not: the two trends coexist in a complicated relationship. The astute contemporary manager is aware of both the radical and logically incommensurable differences between different models of the world that he or she must somehow integrate across *and* of the unreasonably high communicative and persuasive power of certain metaphors and models that have entered modern consciousness. He or she is aware of the possibility of using these communicative tropes to "paper over" the radical differences that stand in need of genuine integration; of the sometimes catastrophic consequences and chronically high costs of such dissimulative attempts; and of the significant successes that have been achieved by focusing the language of technical rationality and first-order optimization on a certain class of tasks: the ones that can be reduced to algorithms.

To produce reliable results efficiently, this cultural-cognitive engine needs, then, one important component, which has been defined, refined, sharpened, and applied to the business world over the past 50 years: the *algorithm,* whose advent (Berlinsky, 2001), implementation, and subsequent development have been an underestimated source of what we call technical progress. To understand the power and appeal of the algorithm at an intuitive level, consider that you have to conduct an industry analysis that will inform the baseline assumptions of a business plan. What starting point for the analysis would make your task most efficient? A loose description of what an analysis entails, using anecdotal evidence from previous cases? A set of guidelines for writing a business plan? A set of instructions for how to write a business plan, structured such that the output from the task prescribed by one instruction forms the input to the task prescribed by the next instruction, and such that the input to the task prescribed by the first instruction is easily accessible?

The power of the algorithm lies precisely in the fact that *it makes efficient the translation of knowledge into action.* As knowledge structures progress in levels of precision and specificity, from "pictures" to "heuristics" to "theories" to "models" to "algorithms," they also become more easily translatable into predictable, output-oriented behavioral patterns, or routines. Not surprisingly, the development of algorithmic *agents*—both human and artificial—has been a natural outgrowth of the recognition of the power and use of the algorithm and a key driver of the decreasing marginal value of algorithmic tasks and skills.

The Decreasing Marginal Value of
Algorithmic Tasks and Skills

Because the algorithm is such an efficient means of turning knowledge into action, much work—attested to by the remarkable predictive success of Moore's law, whereby the computational power of the small-scale engines of algorithmic productions doubles every 2 years—has gone into reducing the marginal cost of algorithmic prowess. The usual focus of discussions of algorithmic capacity and technological prowess is on the evolution of information technology, but we want to focus *directly* on the effect of the proliferation of the algorithm as a cultural and cognitive phenomenon on managerial lifewords, which is the diminishment of the marginal value that can be claimed by carrying out algorithmic tasks, which have become efficiently sub-contractible to algorithmic agents ranging from computers through interactive communication systems to very large scale, low-cost mass-manufacturing organizations that are capital-intensive but labor- and management- lean.

The result of the advent and cultural growth of the algorithm—amounting to what we predict will be referred to as a *algorithmic revolution* that will overshadow the "information revolution" of the late twentieth century—is that managerial work *can* now be efficiently broken down into algorithmic and nonalgorithmic components, which makes it possible to subcontract the algorithmic components to low-cost providers that will keep their costs low by carefully managing the ratio of algorithmic to nonalgorithmic tasks they undertake.

These arguments confront us with the challenge of scrutinizing care-fully the core of contemporary managerial practice and competence: if algorithmic tasks are to be increasingly and with growing efficiency out-sourced, then what do we find there, at the core?

The "Interactions Revolution": Articulating the Tacit to Bridge the Ingenuity Gap

We find *silence*. Johnson, Manyika, and Yee (2005) and Beardsley, Johnson, and Manyika (2006) argue convincingly that the skills of the high-value decision maker of the twenty-first century are *tacit* skills, involved in managing complex interactions among multiple production and exchange agents with different ways of thinking and behaving. Their new kind of worker is a worker skilled at performing activities that are precisely those that *cannot be turned into explicit algorithms* for turning matter into matter or information and knowledge into behavior or matter or information—all of which are what they (somewhat misleadingly) call "transformational" activities (figure 1.3).

By contrast, the high-value decision maker of the future is the man-ager of complex interactions: the manager whose tasks cannot be auto-mated, because, we claim, as the marginal costs and benefits of task automation have decreased to the point at which very high startup costs

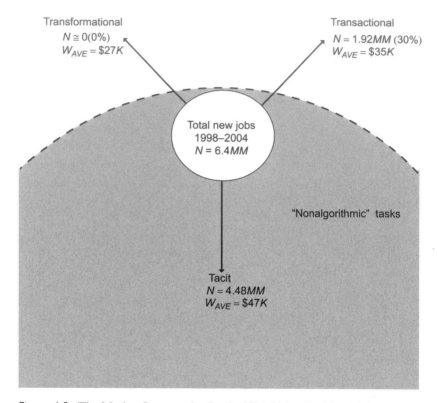

Figure 1.3. The Market Opportunity for the High-Value Decision Maker

can be rationalized, virtually any algorithmically specifiable task can and will—in the end—be automated. The high-value manager's most valuable skills are tacit in the sense that they are not explicit in the same way that the task-specific skills of a production line manager or a development engineer are: they cannot be represented as specified by a set of rules that can be put together into algorithms that reliably turn available inputs into desired outputs.

There are two ways in which we can interpret the tacitness of these tacit skills. The first is to resign ourselves to the notion that these skills can never be made more explicit and therefore can never be developed or selected for. This approach aligns with a lot of the literature that has evolved from the realization that "mind is not (actually) a computer," but only, perhaps, metaphorically so; that there are tasks that we can do that computers can never do (Dreyfus & Dreyfus, 1986); that we will forever outclass computers at solving the metaproblem of problem selection or formulation; but the approach often draws the erroneous conclusion that it is sufficient—as a pedagogical goal—to simply *identify and label* the wicked (nonalgorithmically solvable) problems *qua* wicked problems and tacit skills merely and uniquely as the skills deployed to solve wicked problems and to marvel at our ability to identify this new category of problems in the first place and leave matters at that.

An alternative approach—the one we pursue here—is to attempt to make progress on precisely the wicked problem of identifying and attempting to develop the tacit skills that make a difference to the solution of wicked problems—and thus to engage in the kind of articulation that we have expressed doubts that markets can successfully undertake. These new skills are at present an emergent phenomenon; they are not trained or cultivated. They are often looked on as offering hope for bridging the "ingenuity gap" identified by some as a looming limit to human development (Homer Dixon, 2000), as the (negative and growing) differential between the supply and demand of ideas that can solve the social, economic, technical, and moral problems that we collectively have created. Man-made solutions to man-made problems are in short supply, the argument goes, then stops. We need to take it further.

The nature of tacit skills may be such that the ingenuity gap is not in any sense a quantitative but rather a qualitative one. It is not a know-what gap in numbers of appropriate ideas or of other purely cognitive objects, but rather a gap in know-how-to—in the *cognitive-behavioral modules* required to bridge between fact and value, thinking and action, and among different modes of thinking and being; between different ontologies, different epistemologies, different logics; between different forms of life—all while "retaining the ability to function"—in F. Scott Fitzgerald's resonating formulation. They are enabling personal technologies that allow one to locally and fallibly transform wicked problems requiring constant interpretation and negotiation of the nature and criteria of acceptable solutions into complex or simple problems that can be tackled by the algorithmic processes and procedures that we have created and optimized over the course of four centuries—in fact, since the original development of the Anglo-American accounting system and the increasingly sophisticated technologies for counting and calculating that have culminated in the computer and the Internet (see figure 1.4).

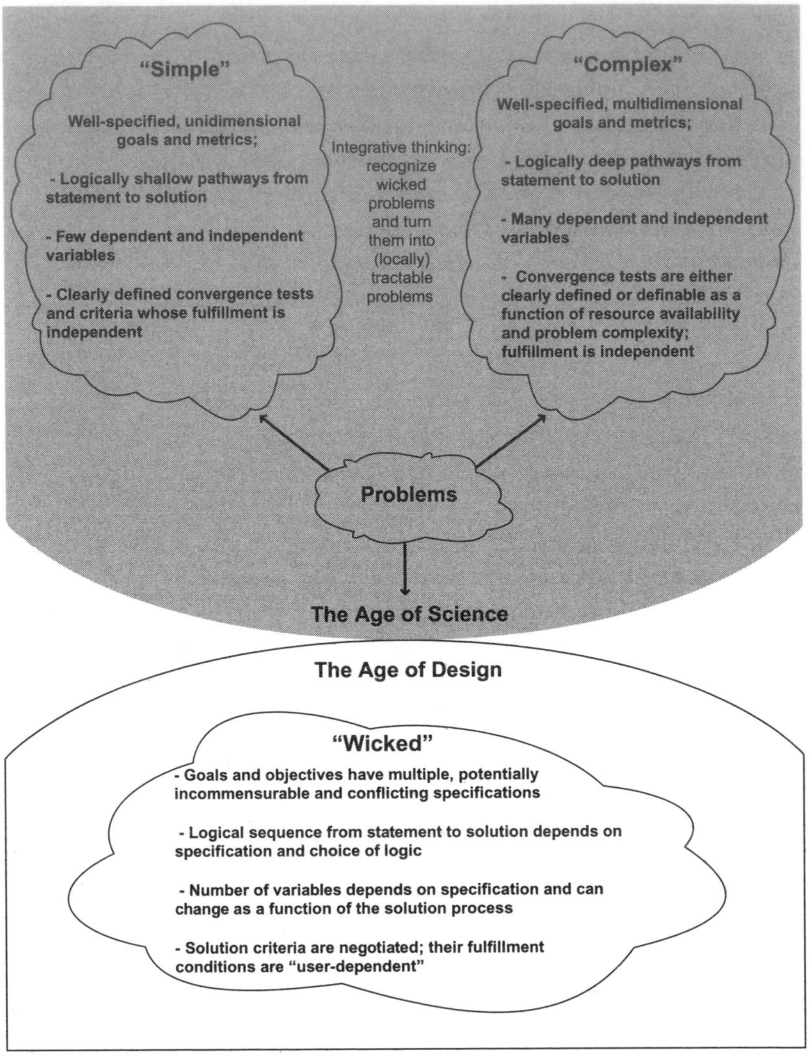

"Simple"

Well-specified, unidimensional goals and metrics;

- Logically shallow pathways from statement to solution

- Few dependent and independent variables

- Clearly defined convergence tests and criteria whose fulfillment is independent

Integrative thinking: recognize wicked problems and turn them into (locally) tractable problems

"Complex"

Well-specified, multidimensional goals and metrics;

- Logically deep pathways from statement to solution

- Many dependent and independent variables

- Convergence tests are either clearly defined or definable as a function of resource availability and problem complexity; fulfillment is independent

Problems

The Age of Science

The Age of Design

"Wicked"

- Goals and objectives have multiple, potentially incommensurable and conflicting specifications

- Logical sequence from statement to solution depends on specification and choice of logic

- Number of variables depends on specification and can change as a function of the solution process

- Solution criteria are negotiated; their fulfillment conditions are "user-dependent"

Figure 1.4. The Problems of the World: A Map

"High-Value Decision Makers": The Predicament of the Manager of the Future

To make progress on the task of articulation we have set for ourselves, consider a considerably simplified example of a critical decision maker—a general manager at a major telecommunications manufacturing firm (such as Cisco, Nokia, Nortel, Alcatel, or Siemens) attempting to bring to market (or *beta release*) a new wireless cellular base station for voice and

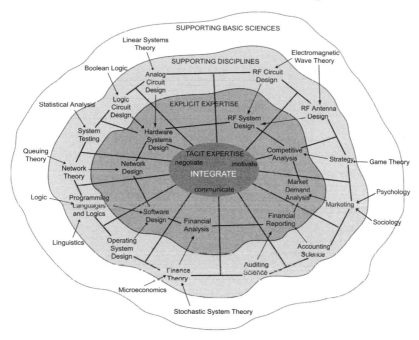

Figure 1.5. Requisite Expertise Map of a General Manager for a Large Telecommunications Equipment Manufacturer

data communications. Even at the purely technical and economic levels, he or she must motivate, monitor, coordinate, negotiate, and argue with experts with disparate disciplinary backgrounds and produce arguments patterned on the underlying logics and discourse ethics of different basic sciences, each based not only on a different vocabulary and technical code drawn from mutually disjoint basic disciplines but also on a different set of *standards of argumentation,* reasoning and interaction and different modes of behavior (see figure 1.5).

An argument about the optimality of a queuing process for the data distribution engine embodied in the base station, for example, will have different standards for closure or resolution than will an argument about market timing and will rely for this closure on a different combination of analytical and empirical reasons than will an argument about market timing. In such a case, deductive logical closure, in the form of an existence or optimality proof, will trump other forms of discursive rationality—such as reasoning by analogy and making extrapolations from prior experiences. If we recall the fundamental epistemological problems surrounding inductive generalizations discussed earlier in this chapter, the "ingenuity gap" that shows up in the clash between areas of expertise becomes understandable as the problem of bridging across different *epistemological stances,* different levels of relative commitment to disparate logics of inference—deductive, inductive, or abductive.

Different domains of expertise—all required for the successful execution of the product—are embedded in fundamentally different logics of inference and also in different *forms* of logic: modal logic—granting epistemic status to *possibilities* rather than only to actualities; declarative logic—denying such status to possibilities and limiting valid inferential bases to actualities, or "facts" and "laws" or "rules" alone; *second-order* logics, allowing statements about statements; *fuzzy* logics, allowing gradations in "true" and "false" predicates; and so forth.

The modal logic of design used by the system architect must be brought—through the medium of our integrator—into dialogue with the declarative-logic-based language(s) of the programmer and the network theorist; the inductive and abductive logics of the marketer, the strategist, and the product line manager must be brought into dialogue with the (deductive) logic of the hardware engineer. Because different disciplines entail not only different communication communities but also different *communities of practice* and modes of interrelating—different standards of punctuality and probity, standards of honesty, transparency, logical auditability and intellectual honesty, standards of sufficient reason and just cause, standards of justification and validation—integrative management in this example requires understanding and impacting the fine mesh of embodied social action norms that rise from the different fields represented in the project.

Successful integration of these different worldviews and modes of behavior and communication is essential to our manager both for building credibility and legitimacy around his or her arguments and actions and for successfully and credibly monitoring and sanctioning the tasks and auditing the arguments of various contributors. As information becomes currency within the organization and task-specific, hard-to-transfer knowledge confers *de facto* decision-making authority on its legitimate holder, the value of the integrator to the organization increases with his or her ability to successfully understand and resolve the fundamental model clashes, tensions, and incongruencies at all levels—logical, ontological, epistemological, behavioral—that emerge among contributors and to competently monitor communities of knowledge that crave autonomy from the fetters of owners and managers. Because knowledge power is sustained by the creation and maintenance of closed hermeneutic circles in which professionals interact in language systems and by using norms of validation and justification that are increasingly difficult to access by outsiders, the high-value decision maker—as the ultimate generalist—must increasingly become a consummate integrator—a task that is nonalgorithmic and falls in the currently "tacit" realm.

The integrator's problem is implicitly familiar to many a business school graduate or academic. Sociologists, economists, and psychologists—exponents of the dominant basic disciplines represented in business school academia—have evolved separate standards of argumentation, inquiry, justification, and validation and separate language systems for representing and communicating about managerial and organizational phenomena, which have evolved in isolation, in a context of specialized communities of knowledge and communication that have come to ask research questions that are very different from one another. Each instantiates its own *hermeneutic circle,* or set of hermeneutic circles, which means that the integrator's problem in the realm of academic discourse can be understood as the problem of constructively bridging across parallel hermeneutic circles. If one is to make sense of these theories taken *together* and to use them for understanding and explaining an organizational phenomenon, one must grapple with the epistemological and ontological problems that we have raised.

Parts of the integrator's problem *have* been articulated—not in any management textbook that we know of but in attempts by a few thinkers to come to grips with the link between words and objects, thinking and doing, perceiving and believing, and believing and knowing. In many cases, as Ghoshal (2005) points out, normative assumptions and injunctions have been inseparably woven into the descriptive fabric of these disciplines, which makes the integrator's problem one of managing normative conflict and tension as much as one of mediating across different universes of discourse.

The integrator's core skills are *tacit* in the sense that they cannot be captured by algorithms and can never be fully explicitly represented. In the chapters that follow, we attempt to show that academic practice *can* supply useful tools for integrators seeking to bridge separate hermeneutic circles on the condition that it recognizes and accepts the tacit dimension of the integrator's expertise and commits to *working* in the tacit domain by attempting to inculcate and develop productive *stances* and *modes of being* as opposed to attempting to disseminate knowledge and information structures that remain isolated from lived experience and action.

The Nature of the Integrator's Production Function

Two features of the integrative function announce themselves in the previous discussion: it is at once (1) necessary and (2) not efficiently outsourced.

1. It is necessary in that the firm as a whole does (more or less well) achieve an integration among different knowledge bases, ways of acting, knowing, communicating, representing, and so forth, in the sense that any global outcome brings together the chain of activities of the firm into *some* causal nexus, *some* denouement. Bankruptcy and failure are *integrative* outcomes; in them, integration of all of the causal chains that make up the four-dimensional object called an "organization" *happens*— even though no one sets out from the beginning to *make* it happen. The manager becomes a high-value decision maker by making integration happen more successfully, by becoming an effective *integrator.*

2. The integration function is *not efficiently outsourced* because the result of outsourcing it is a loss of the full benefit associated with it (along with the contracting costs). Kreps's (1990) analysis of the nonsubcontractibility of the *culture* of the organization, defined by him as a set of stored and commonly known (but often tacitly so) focal points in a set of (often unconsciously played out) coordination games, applies here as well: integration happens largely in the tacit domain and depends for its success on hard-to-specify behaviors. Subcontracting, by contrast, requires an explicit and algorithmic representation of "deliverables" that makes the contract between principal firm and subcontractor a computable function of observable variables (Anderlini & Felli, 1994)—precisely what integration is not amenable to.

Because the problem of integration is at once unavoidable and inescapable, *integrating* appears as a fundamental managerial function. However, it is not, thereby, the easier to describe and analyze— and much damage has been done to its cause to date by considering it a "jack-of-all-trades" or "generalist" skill. In contrast, we posit integration as a specialized skill, thereby incurring the burden of articulating it more precisely.

It is, therefore, useful and timely for the purpose of our analysis to get a little more reductive for the sake of making progress. Call the integrative capacity *the ability to think and act responsibly and responsively in the face of*

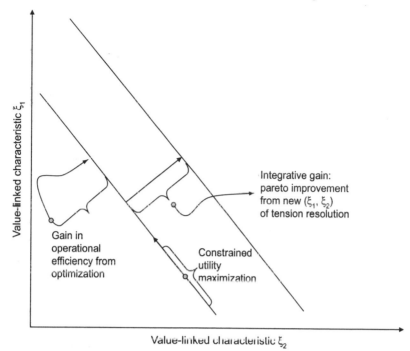

Figure 1.6. The Integrative Function of Management (adapted from Porter, 1996)

multiple, incommensurable, and possibly conflicting models of oneself, the world, and others. To be precise, we have subsumed under the term *models* not only cognitive objects such as theories, schemata, and other representations but also embodied knowledge structures such as modes of argumentation, justification, and personal technologies for understanding oneself and others. The successful integrator builds value through the productive resolution of tensions among such models.

To relate the integrator's function with a well-known picture in the managerial literature, we can modify Porter's (1996) formulation of "strategy" as the achievement of new combinations of inputs, skills, and activities that push outward the Pareto frontier of the organization's production function and claim that successful integration is what the high-value decision maker does to create value beyond the current operational efficiency limit of the organization. By contrast, *pure operational optimization*—instantiated by the pursuit of algorithmic activity sets—can be understood as taking the organization from a suboptimal set of combinations to the operational efficiency frontier (figure 1.6).

The Integrator in Action

Stories can help the enterprise of intellectual entrepreneurship, not by providing validation for conjectures but by helping us articulate a particular phenomenon—the task we have set for ourselves. The stories that follow are not meant to "do science" around the new concept of the integrator, but they are useful for making progress on the problem of articulation, of bringing to language intuitions about a new dimension of managerial being-in-the world that is as yet poorly articulated: for it is articulation that must precede any foundational, qualitative change process, and it is articulation that cannot be relegated to the otherwise very effective market mechanism for aggregating information. Here is how some recent breakthroughs in embodied strategy making instantiate the integrative skill and function:

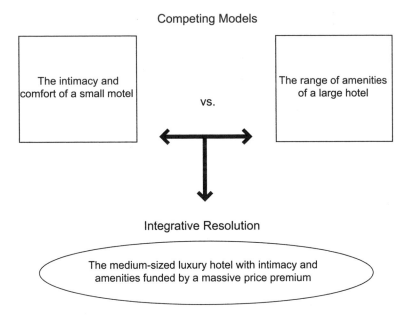

Figure 1.7. Isadore Sharpe, Four Seasons Hotels and Resorts

Isadore Sharpe at Four Seasons   Isadore Sharpe created the Four Seasons experience in response to the seemingly irreconcilable tension between the need to provide the intimacy and comfort of a small hotel with the range of amenities and services and attending economies of scale of a large hotel by designing and rapidly prototyping and perfecting the medium-sized luxury hotel with intimacy and amenities funded by a massive end-customer price premium (figure 1.7).

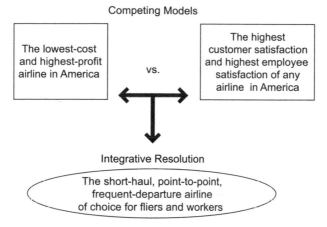

Figure 1.8. Herb Kelleher, Southwest Airlines

Herb Kelleher at Southwest Airlines   Herb Kelleher made Southwest Airlines into the short-haul, point-to-point, frequent-departure airline of choice for leisure and business travelers in response to an articulated aim to simultaneously become *both* the lowest cost and highest profit airline in North America and the highest employee satisfaction airline in North America, a business model that satisfies multiple goals that one usually thinks of trading off quasi-linearly against one another (figure 1.8).

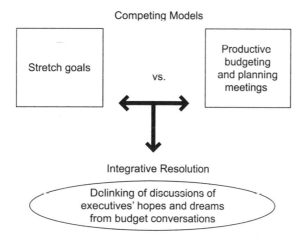

Figure 1.9. Jack Welch, General Electric

Jack Welch at General Electric   Jack Welch resolved the tension between embedding stretch goals in the organization and keeping budgeting and planning meetings efficient and productive by delinking discussions of executives' hopes and dreams from conversations about budget (figure 1.9).

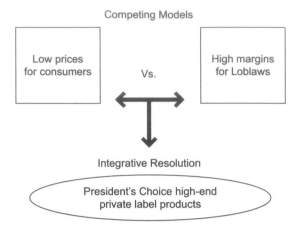

Figure 1.10. Richard Currie, Loblaws Companies Limited

Dick Currie at Loblaws   Dick Currie created the President's Choice high-end private label products as a way of resolving the conflict between the (stated) goals of providing both low end-customer prices and high profit margins for Loblaws (figure 1.10).

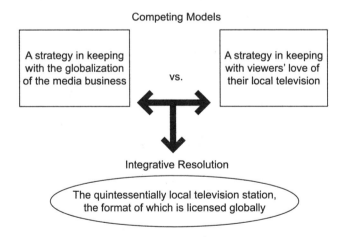

Figure 1.11. Moses Znaimer, CityTV

Moses Znaimer at CityTV   Moses Znaimer made CityTV into the "quint-essentially local" television station—a globally licensed concept success-fully replicated in 22 other countries—as a way of providing a strategy that is responsive to both the globalization of the media business and the yearning of viewers for local feel and content (figure 1.11).

The Integrator's Virtues

If it is the case that an integrative skill is essential to the high-value decision maker—an essential component of the set of tacit skills that will drive value creation in postmodern high capitalism—then it makes sense to ask: What are the new managerial *virtues* that we should aim to select, cultivate, and develop?

We note that the productive resolution of seemingly intractable tension must be rooted in the recognition of different ways of thinking and acting—of *being*, more generally. The "local television station" that Znaimer thinks about is a *microworld*—a community of practice—that is radically different from the cosmopolitan station—another microworld. They entail different patterns of interaction, different capital budgeting constraints, different organizational rule sets, different interorganizational network structures. To integrate successfully, between them one needs the nimble-mindedness to understand the different microworlds *in their radical otherness,* to walk around in them in order to internalize just how deep the tension between them really is. Once the tension has been understood, the integrator requires the big-mindedness to simultaneously behold the competing models. Her or his mind must contain the radical otherness of several different possible worlds that are in tension with one another without falling into paralysis. The creative resolution of the tension is causally related to the accurate comprehension of the tension that must be resolved and understanding that is loyal and fair to each of the opposing models.

Subsequently turning the new insight into action—embodying the idea, producing the revolutionary behavior—requires tough-mindedness, the willingness to try out behavior and allow his or her ideas to die in his or her stead, a quality that bears great similarity to Karl Popper's view (Popper, 1959; 1979) of epistemic rationality *tout court*—and entails the will to carry out the difficult experiments aimed at testing mental objects through attempts at refuting their empirical consequences and discarding those that cannot fruitfully be embodied into organizational action.

Two observations: First, the specific embodiment of these capabilities is *tacit:* they cannot be reduced to rule sets that govern behavior in the sense in which rules of software programming, balance sheet auditing, or options pricing following a certain model can. *Logic,* for instance—which is required to connect facts to the hypotheses that these facts are meant to test and which is thus a key component of any tough-minded decision maker's repertoire—is often thought of as a normative science and taught as a normative dogma, but it is in fact a *tacit skill*. From the propositions "if Socrates is a man, then Socrates is mortal" and "Socrates is a man," one logically infers "Socrates is mortal," but not by first consulting a logic textbook, figuring out the *modus ponens* rule, and applying it to obtain the result. One simply embodies *modus ponens* in one's thinking (Searle, 2001), rather than saying to oneself: "I believe in *modus ponens* and **therefore** I believe that I should infer 'Socrates is mortal' from the beliefs 'Socrates is a man' and 'all men are mortal,'" because the "therefore" that we have boldfaced represents another inference that has to be buttressed by an antecedent belief in *modus ponens*, which sets up an infinite regress. Logical inference is something we *just do* (not something we just *know*), in spite of the fact that it is the "glue" that often holds together our cognitive representations (Searle, 2001). By the same token, there is a *tacit* process that must precede any appropriation of the rules of logic as one's own. No amount of lecturing on the axioms of logic by itself can lead one to make these rules one's own, and to make one embody them in one's everyday mental and verbal behavior.

Going even more deeply in the tacit realm, the ability to take another's perspective—not just cognitively, but down to the ontological and epistemological dimensions of that perspective—a key to the ability to bridge across hermeneutic circles—cannot be specified as a set of rules or as an algorithm. Even though its physiological corequisites and conditions can be understood (Gallese, Keysers, & Rizzolatti, 2004) by the painstaking reconstruction of the neural mechanisms ("excitation of 'mirror neurons'") instantiated when we understand the emotions, thoughts, and behaviors of others, such an ability cannot be inculcated by normative indoctrination ("follow rule set *R* to become more nimble-minded") derived from a set of findings and models stemming from a deeper neurophysiological self-understanding, for the simple reason that we do not know how to issue commands to independent neural centers in the brain.

Second, the fact that we cannot explicitly train these skills (i.e., by enunciating a set of rules that capture the salient parts of the skill, getting trainees to memorize the rules, and giving them arguments for using these rules) does not mean either that we cannot *select* for them or that we cannot attempt to develop them *experientially*, using the tacit realm itself to develop skills that live in the tacit realm. In fact, one way to understand progress in psychological science is precisely by the discovery of reliable, measurable proxies for internal qualities that cannot even in principle be measured. Below we delve only briefly into the problem of selecting for the new skill set; in subsequent chapters we treat the problem of developing these skills at greater length.

Selecting the Integrators of the Future: A Sketch of the MBA's New Selection Function

How can integrative thinkers be selected for? How does the integrative mind-set map into the current state of the art of psychometric and personality testing? At stake is no less than radically increasing the *selection value* of the MBA—the value of the MBA as a selection filter that picks out in advance precisely those future managers who are most likely to become high-value decision makers.

As we argued earlier in our *selection engine model* of the MBA, it is possible to understand postgraduate programs of education in management as selection filters that—given the current educational and cultural environment—are "programmed" to select candidates who have greater general intelligence (*g*) and greater conscientiousness than others—*ceteris paribus;* and it is this particular filtering capability that creates value beyond the development value of the MBA.

It is most likely that general intelligence and conscientiousness will remain significant attributes of the high-value decision maker of the future. Inferential speed and working memory—significant correlates of general intelligence (Gottfredson, 1997) are important enablers and facilitators of the cognitive tasks of the integrator, in the rapid understanding of complex knowledge and information structures, in the rapid decoding and reencoding of difficult-to-understand languages developed by professionals and specialists, and in the rapid design and interpretation of critical tests of theories and mental models.

Conscientiousness, a "big five" personality trait (Goldberg, 1992), can be understood to effectively proxy for the ability of an individual to bind himself or herself to a future action without regard to immediately occurring desires and temptations—and thus can safely be expected to figure prominently in the "value metric" of any decision maker who must act on his or her decisions. For these reasons, the metrics currently in vogue are likely to remain valuable as selectors and can be used as constraints in the design of new selection filters. The question remains: The maximization of *what* can these constraints usefully constrain?

Divergent Thinking, Open-Mindedness,
and "Open-Beingness"

A natural psychometric projection for nimble-mindedness and big-mind-edness is the set of capabilities normally referred to in the literature by the terms *lateral thinking, divergent thinking,* and *open-mindedness* (see, for instance, Eysenck, 1985, for discussion of correlation of such measures with significant creative achievement). Significant work in cognitive and social psychology has gone into understanding both the processes and mechanisms for closure of the mind and ways of measuring an individual's relative proclivity to seize on a particular belief, theory, model, or metaphor simply as a result of exposure or in response to aversion to randomness and unpredictability and to freeze on that mental object even in the presence of anomaly or disconfirming evidence (see Kruglansky & Webster, 1996, for a review). Accordingly, cognitive measures of open-mindedness (which include lateral and divergent thinking) are useful not only as proxies for big and nimble minds but also as indicators of the marginal proclivity of individuals to avoid well-known belief confirmation and justification biases (see, for instance, Abelson, 1986) and proclivities to alter or delete anomalous data that conflict with a closely held theory or model (Greenwald, 1980), that is, as proxies for a key element of tough-mindedness, which is the ability to recognize refuting or disconfirming evidence.

Is cognitive openness the best that current psychometric science can do relative to our goal of increasing our chances to pick out integrators from the self-selected pool of applicants? If we focus on the ability of the high-value decision maker to bridge incommensurable models and modes of interaction, we realize that cognitive breadth is helpful, for it helps one engage with *different* cognitive structures, but it does not address the ontological and epistemological dimensions of the differences one hopes to bridge. What is needed is a more comprehensive measure of openness, one that picks out preferential access to more open modes of being rather than just the ability to "think in different languages, images, or models." Here, the common cognitive approaches of psychometric science fall short—a failure that has led many to posit other intelligences (Gardner, 1993) and other modes of deploying the intelligence one has (Sternberg, 1985)—but separate lines of inquiry into *empathic accuracy* (Ickes, 1997) have yielded measurement scales that turn the quality of being able to relate to emotional states and comportments of others that are radically different from one's own—or that fall outside of one's own repertoire of behaviors and emotions—and that have received independent validation from neurophysiological studies as phenomena backed by a neural apparatus that is separate from the prefrontal cortical engine associated with cognitive function (Gallese et al., 2004). *Ontological openness,* therefore, can be given a psychometric projection, one which, coupled with established measures of open-mindedness—in the purely cognitive sense of "mind"—provide a psychometric foundation for selection mechanisms that seek out big and nimble minds.

"Egonomic Potential" and Executive Function

Is conscientiousness the best we can do as a leading indicator of ability to act in the face of radical incommensurability and model clash in designing a selection filter for the decision makers of the future? We do not think so. Here is why: what we are after is not merely an ability to bind oneself using reasons, promises, and representations, or to act on duty in the face of temptation, or to "do what one has most reason to do" in the face of short-run temptations. We are, rather, in search of a true *executive function,* which allows the integrator to think two radically different thoughts and not become panicked or paralyzed by the realization that they have different immediate action implications, and to understand two or more different points of view with great fidelity—each in its own sense and each with its own implications for thinking and action—without losing the ability to think critically about each, to create new mental objects that synthesize them, and to design experiments aimed at testing the new mental objects. What might this executive function look like when projected onto the world of what psychologists can measure "from afar" with the blunt tools of surveys and experiments?

A powerful candidate is the self-control "muscle" that Roy Baumeister and his coworkers have posited and refined as a construct that explains individuals' ability to engage in two or more attention-hungry, difficult tasks over extended periods of time (Muraven& Baumeister, 2000). To exemplify the workings of this function: individuals instructed to abstain from eating immediately accessible sweets have greater difficulty remaining focused on attempting to solve difficult puzzles than individuals who do not have to actively control a temptation, and this difficulty increases as a function of time spent trying to carry out both tasks (abstention and reasoning) together. Individuals who engage in solving a difficult puzzle while controlling a temptation fare more poorly when they subsequently have to solve a different puzzle than do individuals who did not have to engage in a complex self-control maneuver.

Just as in the case of a muscle, however, performance in two-task self-control processes can be enhanced through the performance of periodic self-control exercises—such as directed postural changes. This executive function can be extended to the realm of thought control, as well—following the suggestion of Schelling (1984) of the mind as an "organ that can (usually) not control itself"—and posited as a unique ability of the mind to direct itself to think in particular ways. This can be understood as a critical component of the "big mind" that can believe and understand several radically different models or theories without immediately or compulsively committing to any one of them. What emerges from this line of inquiry is a potentially powerful composite measure of executive function—or "egonomic potential," the ability to manage the intrapsychic processes of the self—that can be calibrated to discern individual differences in integrative capacity. To be sure, most "evidence" about the average human's ability to control his or her own mind is pessimistic (Wegner, 1994) for reasons that psychologists have been quick to build models around, but no less certain is the glaring fact of large individual differences in the all-important function of "mind-shaping," differences that await both exploration and exploitation.

What has to happen in order for such selection metrics to be designed into the selection mechanisms that filter admission to programs of higher education and training in business? First, the selection value of the MBA and the value of admissions-based selection both to the overall selection mechanism and to the development value of the MBA have to be recognized. The MBA *already* is a selection mechanism, albeit an imperfect one, shaped by inertia and institutional forces that have little to do with the problem of finding and developing the high-value decision makers of the future. Designing new and improved selection metrics into the selection process does not change the status of the MBA, turning it from a development program into a selection program; it simply builds and improves on the already present state of affairs, as interacting with other high-self-command, highly divergent thinkers adds to the educational experience of the program.

Second, the task of designing selection mechanisms based on valid studies correlating individual-level characteristics with desired managerial abilities and performance levels has to be invested in. For example: experimental measures of executive function will either need to be implemented within admissions processes—leading to more complex admissions procedures—or new and difficult-to-game inventories, similar to personality inventories, will need to be developed, calibrated, and refined. A large IQ-and-conscientiousness-based selection machine such as that inhabiting the core of modern higher education has taken many decades to implement and hone, and there is significant status quo bias that will make change difficult. However, given the nature of the MBA as a selection engine and the increasing importance of skills and abilities that transcend the "algorithmic nexus" of IQ and conscientious-ness, we predict that the payoffs to making these changes in a decisive fashion will be significant for those who have the vision and courage to undertake them.

2

Business School 2.0

Can the Contemporary Scientific-Educational Complex Educate the Manager of the Future?

We have seen the enemy, and he is us.
Walt Kelley, Pogo

Business academics are—*right now*—well equipped to develop and culti-vate the integrator's qualities and virtues in their students; the tools and practices for doing so are already in place. However, the ethos and the institutions of business scholarship and teaching must be understood in a new light and redeployed in virtue of this new understanding in order to capitalize on the opportunity that the existing social and intellectual landscape of business academia presents.

Here is a sketch of the argument: first, the epistemological and ontic pluralism of business research activities creates a favorable breeding and proving ground for tough-, nimble-, and big-minded thinkers.[1] The para-digmatic mental models of the different core disciplines "come together" in business schools—and this presents them with a unique opportunity for developing the inner-conflict-competent thinker and doer. What is needed is a reconceptualization of substantive, epistemological, and ontic

---

1. The difference between *ontic* and *ontological* is worth explaining here briefly. The *ontological* dimension relates to the entities that one takes to be real, where *takes* denotes more than just a cognitive understanding: they are the entities that one acts toward as if they were real, and which often one makes real through these very actions. The *ontic* dimension relates to the *categories* that one uses to understand the world, the concepts one uses to make sense of evidence, data, and the like. Not surprisingly, academics often work with the *ontic* dimension—they articulate cognitive schemata for understanding various data sets, but these concepts do not always form ontologies; few are those academics who *live* out their theories. The distinction is due to Martin Heidegger (1927).

tension and conflict—the very "stuff" of what academics often refer to as "paradigm wars"—as fundamentally a productive phenomenon, one to be brought forward in new pedagogical experiences aimed at legitimating the experience of the conflict or tension. The nimble-minded manager can come to walk around in the shoes of *homo economicus, homo psychologicus,* or *homo sociologicus,* and in the end become big-minded by feeling *comfortable* along the way of this walk. The self of the nimble-minded manager grows through confrontation with other possible selves that cannot be reduced to a single entity—and through a visceral, as well as cognitive and comportmental, understanding of this irreducibility.

Furthermore, the *tough-minded* manager can be understood to act out a version of the sophisticated methodological falsificationism that Imre Lakatos (1970) posited as a neo-Popperian logic of scientific discovery—one that gets around the technical problems (Miller, 1994) associated with Popper's original (1959) approach to defining "method" in science yet is a better descriptive model for what the intellectually honest scientist *actually does* than are its precursors. It is a falsificationism-for-the-thinking-doer—who must, at the end of "thinking" and "trying out," make a *choice* among competing theories in the face of multiple, plausible alternatives in the interpretation of any data set. Given the self-understanding of academics as falsificationists guided by a refutation-centered logic in their tasks as designers of experiments and quasi-experiments, all that is required for a (mimetic) transfer of this valuable skill to students is for the educators to "walk their own talk" in the classroom and embody the model they espouse in the *actual* ways they search, research, and teach. The shift from "knowingness" to "unknowingness," from "scientisticity"—the simulated *appearance* of rigor—to scientificity, from justificationism to falsificationism, is not altogether straightforward to bring about, for reasons that we discuss later; but the requisite "hardware" exists and the "software" required to configure it is at hand.

Obstacles to Ontic and Ontological Pluralism: Two Forms of Departmentality and the (New) Structure of the Market for Ideas

We begin with a critique of old and new forms of departmentalism in business schools and discuss the specific challenges they pose for the development and cultivation of the integrative, high-value decision maker. An examination of "Business School 1.0" ("released" in 1908 with the foundation of the Harvard Business School) reveals an organization of teaching and research that mimics the functional structure of the business organization (figure 2.1). There are "problems of production," "problems of accounting," "problems of finance," and so forth, to be handled by methods specific to each individual problem area. Business cases come presorted into "productions cases," "operations cases," "finance cases," and so forth: the label is critically important, as it groups likes with likes in terms of business situations and preconfigures the mind of the student to deal with specific areas beforehand.

John Ralston Saul has cogently argued that the labeling process (coupled with the rationalist discourse that places basic categories outside of the realm of what is discussable and negotiable) strips away the richness of situational detail from the predicaments with which future MBAs are confronted as "prototypes" of real business situations (Saul, 1992) and that this loss of detail leads to the "technocrat's illusion" that the world is nothing but a straightforward instantiation of a single and often algorithmically simple mental model. This mental model may be a purely economic view of human behavior (the "finance" mind-set), a computationalist view of human reasoning (the "operations" mind-set), a behaviorist—stimulus-response—view of human motivation (a Skinnerian version of the "human relations" mind-set), or a combination of models that "work well together" because they are used in disparate domains of activity and experience with a rule that says: "never use more than a single model in the same experiential domain" and a meta-rule that says "never question the rule."

As some have argued (Mintzberg, 2004, for instance), the monoparadigmaticity of the individual silos of Business School 1.0 is what flattens out detail. Detail always stands out against a background of relevance

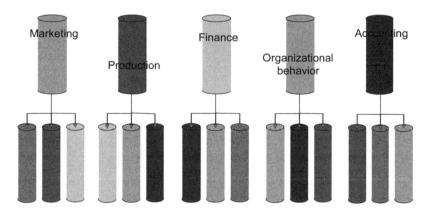

Release date: Harvard Business School, 1908

Figure 2.1. Business Education: Version 1.0

and salience: different facts about an "organizational behavior" case study would stand out in relief in a finance-oriented discussion of the same case than they do in "organizational behavior class." The "ethical" dimension of a "productions case" does not fit into the framework of the dialogue carried out in "productions class"—an "ethics" class, of course, discusses an altogether *different* set of cases, many of which *do* have productions-relevant details that, however, do not get discussed in that class. Each silo conjointly develops rules of thumb for adequate contributions to classroom and scholarly discussions and (often inductively derived) "laws of business" that are (sometimes) used to buttress the rules of thumb in question. True tension has little opportunity to flourish in this setting. In particular, there is no room for:

> *Ontic pluralism:* the simultaneous understanding of multiple, incommensurable cognitive models or images of the organization, the manager, or society at large.
>
> *Epistemological controversy:* tensions among alternative ways of creating knowledge, validating beliefs, or auditing theoretical claims to validity.
>
> *Ontological insecurity:* anxiety caused by doubts about the foundational categories that one feels able to "cut the world at the joints" with (Nozick, 2002).
>
> *Logical pragmatism:* the self-consciously instrumental deployment of multiple logics—descriptive, modal, tensed, untensed, second order—and modes of inference—deductive, abductive, inductive—as structuration devices for thinking and arguing.
>
> *Discursive experimentation:* the trying out of different kinds of communicative behavior and action—verbal and nonverbal—in the classroom, meant to expand the communicative repertoire of the student.

These are precisely the core characteristics of *model clash* situations, the very clash that is prevalent in the contemporary business world, in which predicaments do not come packaged as specialized problem statements and it is up to the decision maker to adjudicate among radically different approaches—and which we have identified as beneficial to developing the important process of integration. Introducing the recognition, enactment, and understanding *model clash* as a consciously pursued pedagogical goal in the Business School 1.0 model would go some way toward alleviating Saul's "technocratic abduction of reality" problem embodied in his "Voltairian bastard" (Saul, 1992): for multiple lenses brought to bear simultaneously on the same case would make *more* details of each case stand out against the new and richer background of relevance. It is, however, against the background of Business School *2.0* that our discussion of model clash takes on an even greater significance.

Fast-forward now to the mid-1970's, to give the Ford Foundation's funding strategy aimed at making business education more "scientific" some time to take effect: Business School 2.0 (figure 2.2) is a structure that is departmentalized similarly to that of Business School 1.0, with the exception that the silos are buttressed by basic social sciences—such as economics, psychology, and sociology. Not all basic sciences are in contact with all disciplines, of course; quite the contrary is the case: transfer of ideas, methods, and concept occurs only where there is already a common "code" that enables communication between the donor basic science discipline and acceptor business discipline. The axiomatic discursive systems of rational choice and rational belief theory, for instance, function as a code that is shared between finance and microeconomic science and that allows ideas from microeconomics to be used in finance theory without the messy (and fundamentally ambiguous) process of interdisciplinary translation. The language of microeconomics, by contrast, is suspect to cognitive and social psychologists teaching organizational behavior courses and to sociologists teaching strategic management because of its Friedmanian "anti-realism" (Friedman, 1953); the functional disciplines that result are, consequently, also foreign to the "ethic of axiomatization" and to the axiomatic approach to understanding behavior that

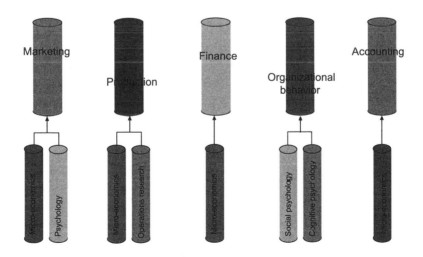

Release date: 1960–1970

Figure 2.2. Business Education: Version 2.0

confers logical auditability on economic models of behavior and thought (Saloner, 1991/1994).

The basic conceptual strategy—"simplify and specialize"—of the social sciences is accepted in the new Business School 2.0 functional silos of business academia, where the—again, messy and indeterminate—processes of conceptual articulation, reduction, and elimination are effectively "subcontracted" to the basic disciplines (economics, psychology, sociology). The complex, ambiguous object that goes by the name of "organization" is reduced, for instance, by different monoparadigmatic approaches—such as conflict sociology, neoclassical economics, modern agency theory—to simple descriptions—such as "hierarchy," "market failure," "nexus of contracts," respectively—that allow narrowly defined research programs held together by core assumptions and basic "empirical questions" to flourish (figure 2.3).

The complex, ambiguous object "person" is appropriated by various disciplines—economics, behaviorist psychology, neuropsychology—that build their practices on simplified representations of personhood ("nothing but a set of preferences and choices" (economics), "nothing but a set

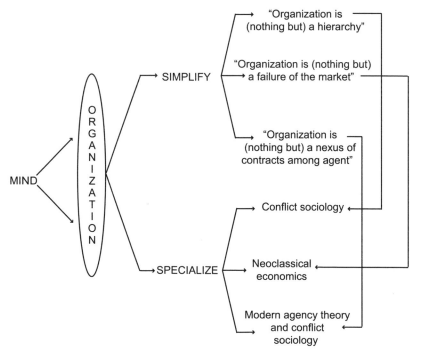

Figure 2.3. Simplification and Specialization around Complex Object "Organization"

of conditioned responses" (behaviorist psychology), or "nothing but a set of causally connected neurophysiological events" (neurobiology) (figure 2.4).

The search for "invariants of human behavior" (Simon, 1990)—or of organizational behavior, or of human behavior in organizations or markets—achieves a unification of sorts among the various functional disciplines as a more or less falsificationist, nomologically oriented approach pursued with greater or lesser rigor becomes the new standard that confers legitimacy on academic speech acts; but ontic differences and differences in standards of inference and logical depth of reasoning patterns go unnoticed and are not addressed. They become only dimly visible demarcation lines among the basic disciplines and even more dimly perceived demarcation lines among the Business School 2.0 silos that emanate from the basic disciplines. The reason is that, with regard to research, the functional silos are largely "net importers" of ideas from the basic social sciences (see Baum & Dobbin, 2000, for a reference to strategic management)—with the exception of finance, which lives inside the "communicative space" of microeconomics but is no longer a net importer of core ideas from microeconomics but rather a direct user of models and techniques from real number

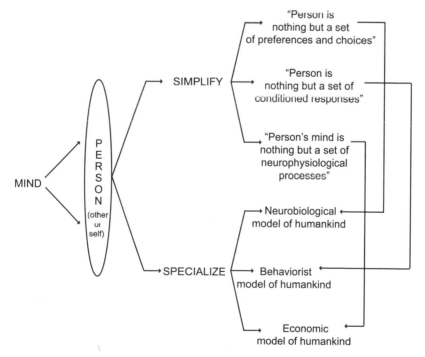

Figure 2.4. Simplification and Specialization around Complex Object "Person"

analysis, combinatorial optimization, stochastic systems theory, statistical mechanics, algorithmic complexity theory, cognitive psychology, and affective neuroscience.

The situation in the new world of Business School 2.0 seems in some respects similar to that of Business School 1.0. There are, to be sure, several "differences" relative to Business School 1.0's environment, but they do not really make a substantial difference:

- The inductive and abductive logic of functional explanation prevalent in the "trade-school" instantiation of the business school curriculum has been largely replaced by the deductive methods and the hypothetico-deductive method for testing theoretical explanations.
- The use of experimental and quasi-experimental methods for validating theories and beliefs are de facto "gold standards"—and good cards to play in legitimation contests inside the classroom and in academic circles.
- The conceptual base of the functional disciplines has been "cleansed" and quite often replaced by the conceptual base of the tributary basic sciences (usually microeconomics, psychology and various strands of sociology).

Most faculty members in Business School 2.0 are trained in doctoral programs that imprint them with the methods and concepts of one (and often only one) of the basic social sciences. In the classroom, they derive legitimacy from the academic studies that they can cite to support a particular opinion and, of course, from the fact that these studies are themselves (still) considered legitimate tokens of validity by their students and thus come to function as *bona fide* tokens of legitimacy. The same faculty members are hard-pressed to come up with answers and to "regenerate a dialogue" when studies from alternative sources or different basic science traditions are deployed to buttress an opposing point of view and also when the theoretical underpinnings of the studies they cite are openly challenged, but their discomfort is often limited to the classroom in which these difficulties are voiced and forgotten afterward. They struggle to formulate prescriptive injunctions that "solve or crack the case" for would-be managers (which have now been codified in popular classroom language as "take-aways") by combining (often hidden) normative approaches to management (most of which remain implicit) with descriptive studies that purport to discover invariant characteristics of "the human mind" or "organizations" or "markets." They get tenure (or not) on the basis of numbers of papers published in journals that are not usually read by practitioners and whose importance is rated and evaluated by academics who are not managers. Their output contributes to the welfare of their schools and departments via the value that rankings of business schools attach to such publications without the benefit of a direct empirical test of the impact of the specific journals' precise content on the "business world." They are "theoretically" aware of the challenges of applying highly simplified and structurally explicit models to understanding human behavior and experience, but have few outlets for voicing these difficulties and little extrinsic incentive to do so. Over time, they become increasingly adept deployers and users of arguments and counterarguments in interactions with peers and students. Because of the strong civilizing force of hypocrisy, they remain on the right side of academic dishonesty, even as they seem to fall ever short of an internal standard of intellectual honesty.

However, there are also encouraging signs in the world of Business School 2.0, signs that, taken together, amount to the seeds of a new way of teaching and researching business:

1. First, the new business academia is now a self-consciously multi-paradigmatic discipline, and this awareness makes it into a *pluri*paradigmatic (even though not yet a *trans*paradigmatic) discipline. Its collective consciousness and conscience is heavy with the recent memory of "paradigm wars" punctuated by reasoned attempts to narrow the epistemological and conceptual foundations of the discipline (Pfeffer, 1993) or, to keep it broad (Van Maanen, 1995), by textured discussions of its epistemological foundations and ontic commitments (McKelvey, 1997) and by an understanding of the misunderstandings and misattributions that these discussions have fostered (Moldoveanu & Baum, 2002). Ontological relativity (McKelvey, 1997) (or, more accurately, *ontic pluralism*) is accepted and encouraged even by those who want to restrict the admissible range of epistemological regimes in which "knowledge" is pursued. The *communicative* and *coordinative* functions of academic language in professional business organizations are beginning to be recognized, in conjunction with its purely representational functions (Astley & Zammutto, 1992). The political functions of disciplinary language and the intimate connection between "is" and "ought" in the models used to represent people, organizations, and markets have been cogently signaled (Ghoshal, 2005)—along with the rich and hidden moral scaffolding in which theories that purport to merely "describe" the world are embedded. A foundation therefore exists for carrying out dialogues that transcend the boundaries of the narrowly construed basic science disciplines. These dialogues and the research that they have generated have already brought into sharp relief the depth and quality of the tensions between alternative models of humans and organizations, the relative value of

"theory," "evidence," "method," and "conceptual framework" in the adjudication of claims to validity, and have helped to elucidate the cognitive commitments of those working in the tradition of various "basic social sciences." As a result, a "fabric" for training integrative thinkers exists; but utilizing it productively requires reconceptualizing ontic and epistemological forms of pluralism as a potential solution and an opportunity, rather than a problem.

2. Second, the disciplinary straitjackets of the existing basic science disciplines are being vigorously challenged by the realization that they are themselves net importers of ideas from a set of "generative sciences" (analytic philosophy, evolutionary and coevolutionary theory, real analysis, complexity theory, hermeneutics, theoretical physics; see figure 2.5)

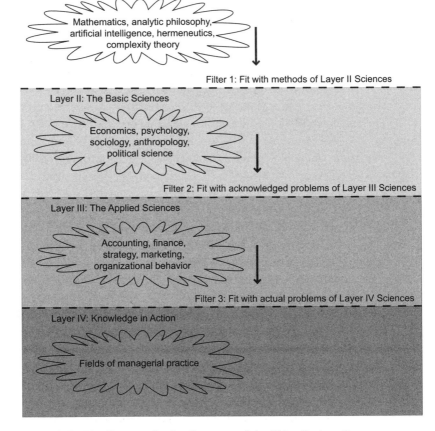

Layer I: The Generative Sciences

Mathematics, analytic philosophy,
artificial intelligence, hermeneutics,
complexity theory

Filter 1: Fit with methods of Layer II Sciences

Layer II: The Basic Sciences

Economics, psychology,
sociology, anthropology,
political science

Filter 2: Fit with acknowledged problems of Layer III Sciences

Layer III: The Applied Sciences

Accounting, finance,
strategy, marketing,
organizational behavior

Filter 3: Fit with actual problems of Layer IV Sciences

Layer IV: Knowledge in Action

Fields of managerial practice

Figure 2.5. The Communicative Structure of the "Idea Business"

and therefore that business scholarship is not necessarily *ontically beholden* to the basic sciences—economics, psychology, sociology—just as they are not *epistemologically beholden* to any one tradition for creating and validating beliefs but rather free to choose and sculpt its foundations in ways that are as responsive to the "practical problems of business" as to the intellectual heritage of several different basic science fields. Paradigmatic pluralism extends to the realm of theories, models, and metaphors for representing the self and the world. New disciplines—organizational neuro-psycho-socioeconomics, the Boolean-network-model (NK(C)) approach to modeling value chains and their linkages, the new science of organizational network dynamics based on the theory of random graphs, the affective neuroscience of financial behavior, the economics and psychoeconomics of linguistic conventions, managerial semiotics, and managerial phenomenology—are taking root in *business schools* without having gone through the apprenticeship of successive years or decades of validation in the antechambers of the traditional social sciences. This trend indicates the achievement by business researchers of the epistemological maturity required to take over new concepts and deploy them in imaginative new explanatory schemata without waiting for independent validation from their more "respectable" brethren—the sign of a real appropriation of the "spoils of science."

3. Third, the *performative* dimension of knowledge has recently come to light and prominence among business scholars. Karl Popper's view of social science as "piecemeal social engineering" (Popper, 1961) guided by a stubbornly empirical process of trial and error never came to fruition in the traditional social sciences (concerned with discovering "invariants of human behavior") but rather in the new self-understanding of social scientists as *designers of intelligent behavior* (see Roth, 2003, for an argument and a powerful example from auction design; and Simon, 1969/1986, for a well-known article on the "sciences of the artificial" that is interesting in spite of the fact that Simon himself never practiced the new logic of design he advocates, even though he *studied* it). It took 100 years for the basic idea (Brouwer's fixed point theorem in real analysis) that makes game-theoretic analyses of social interactions possible to "percolate" through the sieves of various social sciences and become a "design tool" for the Federal Communications Commission (FCC) auction of the 1900 MHz Personal Communications Systems (PCS) spectrum. By contrast, it took 20 years for the basic ideas behind the combinatorial optimization of double-matching markets to become embedded in real practice (Roth, 2003), and 10 years for the Viterbi algorithm for decoding Trellis-coded signals—a coding technique that led to a doubling of the capacity of

some wireless communications channels and enabled an efficiency break-through in cellular telephony—to be embedded in wireless modems and (later) in cellular handsets, fueling the large and growing royalty-based revenue stream of Qualcomm, Inc.

Interestingly, the "engineering" approach to the creation and deploy-ment of knowledge is not foreign to Popper's original "logic of scientific discovery" (Popper, 1959): conceptual pluralism, dogged empiricism, and rabid falsificationism pay off—we conjecture—at least as well in the world of organizational and behavioral design as they do in the world of sci-ence. Perhaps it is not fully the case, as J. S. Mill argued, that "the logic of science is the same as the logic of business and the logic of life." But, as Simon (1969/1986) pointed out, the addition of a logical infrastructure that allows for logical *possibility* and the resulting logically possible worlds to play substantial epistemic roles in thinking and deliberation (see also March, Sproull, & Tamuz, 1991, for an argument for allowing *possibility* to count in deliberation)—while the process of *validating solutions* remains essentially the same as that which has worked successfully for empirically minded scientists—goes a long way toward turning scientific thinking into thinking for action. As Charlie Munger (1997) points out, the worldly wisdom embodied in effective business action requires the development of *model checklists*—tests aimed at eliminating false ideas quickly and decisively—a tenet that is obviously consistent with the falsificationist's concern to get his ideas to *die in his stead,* as Popper had put it.

We are faced, then, with a significant opportunity for change in the cultivation and training of the managers of the future that makes use of a lot of good work and resources currently under the control of business schools:

1. We can exploit the conceptual and epistemological self-aware-ness and pluralism and the reasoned dialogue that has emerged around it during the past 10 years in business academia to design educational experiences that develop big and nimble minds, capable of dealing with radical conceptual conflict and used to seeing situations through multiple ontic and epistemological prisms; by bringing such pluralism *into the open* and thus exposing the trainee to the fundamental tensions that arise in attempts to explain, predict, shape, or justify human behavior, the rich back-ground of situational detail that is kept hidden by monoparadig-matic approaches is freed up (often, of course, at the expense of simple "take-aways"); the result is a complexification of the mind that can increase the competence of the decision maker to deal with radical conflict and ontological incommensurability.

2. We can harness the new emphasis in business academia on the use of knowledge as a design tool to create experiences that allow the thinkers of the future the room to experiment with ideas in action, to "live it," to design and devise their own experiments, to engineer their own situations, to appropriate knowledge in the performative realm, and thus to turn the ontic dimension into an ontological dimension. It is not psychological "science"—a dead textbook affair—that is worth imprinting on the thinker of the future, but the mental habits of the tireless designer of experiments for answering questions about human behavior—the (ideal) scientist him- or herself; the tricks that get him or her to *produce* the right effects; the obsessiveness over the "demand characteristic" of the experimental design; the recklessness of the questioning of the original insight. It is not "strategic frameworks" that we should burden the integrative thinker's working memory with in strategy classrooms, but a *generative semantics* for building new models, a basic repertoire of useful mental objects (images, metaphors, systems of coupled equations, relational, kinematic and dynamical schemata, narratives and metanarratives) that can be adaptively deployed to create new models for new situations and a logic of testing these mental objects with an eye to abandoning the ones that "do not work."

3. We can use the (already well developed) falsificationist ethos of scientific inquiry to help cultivate a tough-minded awareness of the fallibility of human enterprise and a willingness to walk on the "uncomfortable side." Empiricism (not the metaphysics that grows on top of it) and falsificationism form the *lingua franca* and the regulative framework of science, and all we need (assuming we practice it) is to teach it in ways that impart it not only to the mind, but to the flesh, to behavior.

If we pursue these opportunities, we will have graduated as a field from "science" to "engineering," from *episteme* through *techne* and *phronesis* to *poiesis*, from the questioning of Being to the prototyping of new forms of Being. If we do not, we are in danger of remaining mongrels: not-quite-competent managers, not-quite-competent psychologists or economists or sociologists, who are nevertheless dependent on competent capitalists and managers for money and on competent social scientists for ideas, forever cautious and tentative lest an already-suspect educational and professional background should be shown up by an unexpected confrontation with a real problem, one calling for either deep knowledge or prescient action.

An Example: Behavioral Decision Theory and the Study of Managerial Cognition

How does one take advantage of the newfound epistemological and ontic breadth of business academia to change the way ideas are developed and validated? If a precise answer is desired, then the question should be addressed to a particular field or subfield, lest the answer remain at the level of unhelpful generalities. To see how disciplinary straitjackets can be fruitfully opened up without the loss of the rigor and precision that represent core capabilities of academia, we consider the case of an increasingly important discipline in business school academia—behavioral decision theory and the study of managerial judgment formation and cognition—with the aim both of retrieving the dogmatic structures that currently seal off the field from significant progress and of identifying opportunities for productively broadening the axiomatic core of the field in a way that makes use of intellectual traditions and concepts that are currently at hand.

Let us start with a sketch of the idea behind the field's research program. As Max Weber (1911) argued, social scientists approach their phenomena via (1) the postulation of a *normative* model of a subject (or organization), (2) the postulation of a set of possible *departures* from that normative model which one could realistically hope to observe in practice, and (3) the description of an actual, observed behavior as the instantiation of a departure from the normative model. Without an a priori model of *what should be*, no coherent theorizing about *what is* is possible. The descriptive project of the social scientist is enabled by the normative nature of his or her a priori. Weber validly deduced from this approach the inescapability of *value-laden-ness* of the social sciences: normative models—in this view—function in the human sciences in the same way that Kantian a prioris—such as space, time, causality—function in the natural sciences and in lay reasoning about "the world."

The history of the study of lay and—later—managerial cognition offers a prototypical example of the Weberian logic of departures from the normative. When we study human judgments behaviorally according to the dominant approach, we postulate a normative model of belief updating in view of evidence (probability axioms); we articulate a set of possible departures from the correct use of these axioms (violation of conjunction rule [Kahneman & Tversky, 1982] or base rate neglect [Tversky & Kahneman, 1980] amounting to a "fallacy" of availability or representativeness); and then we perform experiments that (often) show that subjects violate the normative rules of probabilistic reasoning by exemplifying systematic departures therefrom.

These experiments are then interpreted to mean that the subjects instantiate cases of "irrationality" (Kahneman & Tversky, 1982). However, these interpretations are not unambiguously—and certainly not uniquely—supported by the experiments they are based on (Moldoveanu & Langer, 2002), on two grounds: first, the experimental situations have interpretations that can reasonably exculpate their subjects from charges of irrationality, and, second, the violation of any particular set of rules of empirical reasoning cannot, in itself, constitute an indictment of the epistemic rationality of the experimental subject so long as there are significant open questions regarding just what correct belief formation is (Nickerson, 1996).

Management science is a net importer of theories and models from disciplines, such as psychology, that are deemed to be more "basic." Thus it is not surprising that the study of managerial cognition proceeds by processes similar to those encountered in the history of cognitive psychology. The appropriation of the methods of the mother field proceeds in the study of managerial cognition by one of two steps: by direct use of the *results* of behavioral decision theory as explanatory variables in models of managerial phenomena (such as "cognitive simplification" strategies [Schwenk, 1984] in strategic decision processes or overconfidence "biases" in patterns of strategic decision making [Kahneman & Lovallo, 1994]) and by the *use* of the normative models of cognitive science and behavioral decision making, in conjunction with well-documented deviations from these models to derive *prescriptive* approaches to teaching managers at the MBA and executive levels and to rendering process and strategic consultation. Prescriptive approaches (Bell, Raiffa, & Tversky 1988, Introduction) aim to prescribe managerial behavior in the face of how others "actually" judge a behavior (rather than prescribing it in the face of how others *should* judge or behave).

How could it be otherwise? By two actionable steps: the first requires loosening the cognitive straitjacket of probabilistic, Bayesian normative models in the study of cognition in general and the study of managerial cognition in particular to include alternatives to the standard, probabilistic logic of belief formation that has dominated the field and has been imported from cognitive psychology and behavioral decision theory, without, however, losing the analytical rigor of these approaches. There are *several* reasonable alternatives to the (probabilist, and, even more broadly, inductivist and justificationist) logic of justifying empirical judgments (Lakatos, 1970; Albert, 1985; Popper, 1959, 1973), and these can be reconstructed to provide powerful schemata for doing standard, "Weberian" cognitive science. Bayesian, Fisherian, and Neymanesque models of intuitive statisticians are only a few of the choices available to the trained—and open-minded—student of cognition.

The jury (if one could be provided) is (or would be) still out regarding the all-things-considered optimality of any single logic of inference, and, although it is not quite true that "because anything can happen, anyone can win," there is as of now also no clear winner in the contest for epistemic normativity.

The second step involves a road map for studying managerial judgments that recognizes and exploits the value of insights from—often not conscious or articulate, but highly interesting and successful—practitioners who "chart the unknown" for a living.

There are undiscussed and often hard-to-discuss problems and dilemmas with each of the normative approaches to the study of epistemic rationality, as even a cursory study of the open-problems literature in epistemology reveals (Audi, 1988)—and solutions to these problems, or new approaches that are not plagued by the problems of traditional approaches, may not come from academics working alone behind the cloisters of academic institutions but rather from "field epistemologists" who chart the still-unknown ways in which skilled managers make sense of the unknown and make critical decisions with only limited, foggy, ambiguous, doubtful, and fuzzy information (Klein, 1998) or from insightful practitioners themselves (Munger, 1997).

To bring the discussion into even sharper focus, let us first reconstruct the mechanisms by which certain a priori normative models of cognition have come to be used—to the detriment of plausible alternatives—as exclusive lenses for the study of managerial judgment formation processes and procedures.

Method as Theory: Forces and Influences Shaping the Current Study of Managerial Cognition

Consider the following questions: Why, in the face of powerful challenges to Bayesian inductivism from neo-Kantian epistemologists such as Karl Popper (1959) and Imre Lakatos (Lakatos, 1970), as well as from "inside" inductivist epistemology itself (Howson, 1995), has the "Bayesian statistician" become entrenched as a normative model of belief formation and updating in the study of lay (Dawes, 1998) and managerial (Bazerman, 1995/2002) cognition? Why are cognitive biases and fallacies so often invoked to explain lay (Gilovich, 1991) and managerial (Bazerman, 1995/2002) patterns of judgment and decision making judged as deviations from this Bayesian logic of judgment formation rather than deviations from some other valid epistemology (such as falsificationism [Popper, 1959] of various kinds [Lakatos, 1970; Albert, 1985])? Why are the experimental results that support these biases only understood as deviations from the Bayesian normative logic rather than as instantiations of some other normative epistemic logic (Moldoveanu & Langer, 2002)?

Gigerenzer (1991) and Gigerenzer and Goldstein (1996) argue that the study of lay cognition has congealed around the question *Are people intuitive statisticians?* largely because of the spread of the use of inferential statistics in North American experimental psychology in the 1940s, 1950s, and 1960s. They argue that discovery in this branch of cognitive psychology has proceeded in a way that suggests a tools-to-theories heuristic: the method of inference practiced by psychologists became a *normative* model of the subject. The behavior of experimental subjects could be described in terms of departures from this idealized subject—whose belief formation processes precisely mimicked those of a reasonable, well-trained experimental psychologist. For example, Kelley's (Kelley, 1973) attribution theory assumed that lay minds act like ANOVA statisticians in making inferences about causes from situations or data about situations. Acceptance of the overarching mind-as-intuitive-statistician metaphor was facilitated by the widespread acceptance of inferential statistical methods as forms of justification for the validity of research findings (Gigerenzer, 1991).

Gigerenzer (1991) points out that the inferential statistics courses taught to experimental psychologists do not hint at the differences, conflicts, and tensions that arise *within* inferential statistics, such as those between Neyman and Pearson, those between Neyman and Pearson on the one hand and Fisher on the other, and those between classical statisticians and Bayesian statisticians. Moreover, there is little discussion even in modern textbooks about the tensions between inductive and deductive-falsificationist forms of inference (Moldoveanu & Langer, 2002) that can be used to raise valid objectives and build valid alternatives to the dominant approaches. In the face of the unification of researchers in the field around a single set of standards for judging epistemic validity, the mind-as-intuitive-statistician metaphor became a relatively undisputed a priori for the study of the cognitive proclivities of real people.

It is, however, not clear from Gigerenzer's analysis why the mind-as-Bayesian-statistician metaphor should have won out over other possible normative starting points for describing how the mind works, points which were not unknown to the "early adopters" of the mainstream approach. Although Gigerenzer signals this fact, he considers it as the instantiation of a "double standard," whereby experimental psychologists hold themselves up to one standard (classical, Neyman-Pearson statistics) and lay subjects to another (classical Bayesian inference).

The research program now associated with Kahneman and Tversky originated as a critique by its founders of the axioms of rational belief used by *economists* to produce explanations of human behavior (Tversky & Kahneman, 1986). Since Savage's work on the axiomatic foundations of subjective expected utility theory (Savage, 1954/1972) and Ramsey's work on the inference of degrees of belief ("subjective probabilities") from betting behavior (Ramsey, 1931) had together laid the foundations for an empirical research program into choice behavior that had quickly consolidated the field of economics, probabilistic models of belief formation had come to dominate the representation of the subject in economics, and the Kahneman and Tversky critique was aimed at the dominant representation of reasoning *in economics,* rather than the *most reasonable* such representation, all things considered.

The field of behavioral decision theory was born—and bred apart from mainstream cognitive psychology at an uneasy boundary between economics and psychology—by the intersection of two ways of doing research: one based on assuming—without empirical investigation—that people *do* act like inductivist, probabilistic inference engines when making judgments, the other based on taking the "mind-as-intuitive-statistician" metaphor as a *normative* point of departure and trying to characterize its actual working as suboptimal departures from this starting point. Together, these two streams of thought generated the rich and fruitful literature on the "availability heuristic," the "conjunction fallacy," the "disjunctive bias," and the "familiarity bias" that together instantiate the "negative" research program articulated by its founders (see Kahneman, Slovic, & Tversky, 1982), which aimed to uncover the ways in which lay cognitive proclivities would differ from those of a rational Bayesian actor informed about and obedient to the axioms of probability and Bayes's theorem.

The mind-as-intuitive-statistician metaphor rode to success in cognitive psychology and behavioral decision theory on the back of the experimental mind-set among psychologists just after the halfway point of the last century. The experimental method became the preferred way of doing psychology (see, e.g., Gigerenzer et al., 1989), inferential statistics became the dominant way of justifying claims to scientific validity (Gigerenzer, 1991), and the mind-as-intuitive-statistician was accepted in the absence of (1) any other well-established metaphor or model and (2) any challenges to the dominant form of inferential statistics.

But why did the mind-as-Bayesian-statistician metaphor become equally entrenched in the field of managerial cognition as (1) an *explanans* for stylized facts about managerial decision making and (2) a point of departure for the study of managerial cognitive proclivities (e.g., Kahneman &

Lovallo, 1994)? Just as the "experimental mind-set" was critical to the establishment of the "mind-as-intuitive-statistician" metaphor in cognitive psychology, the "clinical" mind-set was critical to the establishment of the "mind-as-Bayesian-statistician" metaphor in the study of managerial cognition. The clinical mind-set is based on a mental model of the management scholar or consultant whose main aim is to solve problems faced by managers (including problems *with* these managers and the ways in which they make critical decisions) in a way similar to the work of a clinical physician who aims to heal patients of particular "conditions." The "manager-as-patient" (or organization-as-patient) metaphor became an important part of the decision theorist-as-clinician metaphor. Accordingly, we find many of the contributions to the managerial judgment and decision-making literature (Bazerman, 1995; Dawes, 1998) representing experimentally observed departures from the normative "mind-as-Bayesian-statistician" model of cognition (which, as we saw, served only as a starting point in the greater field of cognitive psychology) as "errors" of judgment *tout court*, a move that was carefully and scrupulously avoided by the framers of the "biases and fallacies" research program, Tversky and Kahneman.

The task of the scholar and instructor is—then—to help those who commit these errors identify them as errors and learn to avoid them in their daily thinking. Just as the mind-as-intuitive-statistician metaphor was useful in creating a large-scale empirical research program in cognitive psychology, the mind-as-Bayesian-statistician metaphor served to spawn a large-scale research program in the study of managerial cognition aimed at (1) identifying managerial biases and fallacies in judgment as deviations from the normative logic, (2) explaining managerial choice behavior as instantiations of such systematic departures from rationality, and (3) attempting to change fallacious patterns of reasoning through education about the correct (Bayesian, inductivist) way of forming and updating beliefs.

The clinical mind-set among scholars of managerial cognition was strongly buttressed by a clever discursive move made by Howard Raiffa (Bell, Raiffa, & Tversky, 1988) by which he argued that decision theorists should offer neither purely normative nor purely descriptive models of the ways in which people should choose or actually do choose among various beliefs, respectively, but rather *prescriptive* models thereof: models that prescribe how someone *should* make judgments given how they and others actually *do* make these judgments.

The *prescriptive* academic, like the clinician, uses experimental findings from cognitive psychology and the research methods of the behavioral decision theorist with a pedagogical intent: given that he or she knows the "right way" to update a set of beliefs given new evidence—and,

therefore, given that there is no meaningful debate about the foundations of epistemic competence—and given certain observed patterns of
judgment that deviate from this "right way," the scholar of managerial
judgment formation should (1) attempt to correct evident biases and fallacies in members of his or her audience and (2) teach these people how
to exploit such biases and fallacies in others. For instance, given that
efficient market hypothesis rests on some—often unspoken—assumptions about the epistemic rationality of traders in the market, teaching
would-be traders how to exploit the biases that others exhibit in making
their trading decisions pushes the market toward greater levels of efficiency in the long run and creates significant above-average returns for
the informed exploiters in the short run.

This approach—simple, persuasive, and well matched to the predicament of the business school academic—nevertheless imposes some
limitations on the range of possible models that can be used to investi-
gate managerial cognition or to articulate new facts about managerial
cognition because it rests on only one normative foundation: Bayesian
inductivism, coupled to the axioms of the probability calculus. However,
the range of experimental facts on which behavioral decision theory and
much of the study of managerial cognition rest admits of many different interpretations—some based on alternative epistemological commitments that (1) are "normative" and (2) exculpate subjects from the charge
of epistemic irrationality—or the commission of "fallacies" in reasoning.
The increase in the level of ambiguity regarding what the experimental
evidence "really" shows about the lay mind, however, is compensated for
by a significant increase in the range of possible models we could use to
study managerial cognition in the field, as well as the laboratory, and
in the level of precision and insight that some of the new models afford
researchers.

Ambiguity, Freedom, and Choice: An Epistemologically
(More) Informed Picture of the Current "State of Play"

Many empirically fruitful research programs owe their achievements to
the consolidation of a field of researchers around a core set of ideas or
models that enable efficient and reliable dialogue (Moldoveanu, 2002),
and the study of managerial cognition through the lens of Bayesian
epistemic rationality offers a good case in point. Arguably, without a
normative model of managerial cognition to guide both empirical investigation and prescriptive theorizing, it may have been difficult for a multitude of researchers to coordinate their activities to the point of creating
a quasi-paradigmatic system of research activities and theories—the

essential underpinning of "normal" scientific practice (Kuhn, 1962). On the other hand, the coming together of research efforts around the mind-as-Bayesian-statistician metaphor led to a narrowing of the possible focus of the study of cognition to a very small subspace of possible models of thinking-for-action.

Field-defining experimental results in the study of cognition (such as the "Linda" experiment [Kahneman & Tversky, 1982] exemplifying a "conjunction fallacy") can admit of several "competing" explanations, some implying "cognitive competence" and some implying "cognitive incompetence" on the part of the subject. There is, thus, hardly a "matter of fact" in the "state-of-the-art" of epistemological debate regarding various inductivist and noninductivist approaches to the formation of updating of beliefs. Therefore, there is no a priori ground for restricting the study of managerial cognition to studies that can be pursued through the currently dominant metaphor, as we illustrate presently.

Tversky and Kahneman (1982) gave participants to an experiment the task to rank, in order of truth-values or personal degrees of credibility, different statements that could be true of a person of whom it is also true that "she is 31 years old, single, outspoken and very bright. She majored in philosophy. As a student, she was deeply concerned with issues of discrimination and social justice, and also participated in anti-nuclear demonstrations." The statements ranged from "she is a bank teller" through "she is a bank teller who is active in the feminist movement" to "she is a psychiatric social worker." Respondents regularly assigned higher truth values to the compound statement "she is a bank teller who is active in the feminist movement" than to the simple statement "she is a bank teller." The authors used these response patterns to infer that respondents' reasoning process seemed to violate the laws of probability, which require that, if A logically implies B, then $P(A) \leq P(B)$. They write, "like it or not, 'B' cannot be more probable than 'A and B,' and a belief to the contrary is fallacious. Our problem is to retain what is useful and valid in intuitive judgments, while correcting the errors and biases to which it is prone."

Here are, however, several exculpatory explanations based on alternative models that can lay at least *prima facie* claims to soundness.

A Popperian Interpretation   Karl Popper (1959) argued for an approach to scientific knowledge in which there is no inductive support for a statement. Taking as a point of departure David Hume's argument that there is no logical basis for induction, Popper argues that scientists (1) should seek information that could falsify their theories rather than verify them and (2) that they should choose from among competing theories those that have (a) the greatest empirical content that has received (b) the most severe empirical tests and (c) has most successfully passed them. If a theory is formed by the conjunction of two falsifiable propositions, A and B, then it will have greater empirical content than a theory which comprises A alone (Popper, 1959). Moreover, if one of A and B have been tested against some observation statement D, then the theory made up of A and B will be preferable to a theory made up of two untested empirical propositions C and D. The consequence of this argument is that one is usually advised to choose, as most likely to be true, the a priori least likely proposition that has survived the most rigorous empirical testing, since a priori the empirical content of "A and B" will be greater than the empirical content of A or B alone, whereas the a priori probability of "A and B" will be less than or equal to the probability of either A alone or B alone. This negation of probabilism is consistent with Popper's insistence that the prior probabilities of law-like universal generalizations is zero (Gemes, 1997). Let A represent "Linda is a bank teller" and B represent "Linda is active in the feminist movement." By a falsificationist account of participants' reasoning, the conjunction "A and B" will be chosen over A—because (1) it has greater empirical content and (2) B has already been "tested" against D, the description of Linda—than the proposition A alone. This interpretation of cognitive processes underlying a famous experiment has even more dramatic implications than the former: the "intuitive scientist"—so much maligned in sociopsychological studies of inference (Nisbett & Ross, 1980; Gilovich, 1991)—may be more of a scientist, by the Popperian account of science, than the scientists administering the tests of scientific competence.

A Psycholinguistic Interpretation   Assume that participants parse the statement "Linda is a bank teller who is active in the feminist movement" as a straight conjunction of the two propositions, "Linda is a bank teller," and "Linda is active in the feminist movement." In first-order logic, the conjunction "A and B" is identical to the conjunction "B and A." In natural language, however, this is hardly the case— indeed, asymmetry of conjunctive sentences is singled out by Dawes (1988) as the reason why we should be cautious of applying probability measures to "language-dependent" representations. "I bought a machine gun and went to the market" is not understood to be identical to "I went to the market and bought a machine gun." In language, conjunction is asymmetric. Moreover, the fact of a conjunction may change our interpretation of the terms in the conjunction. "I bought a machine gun" in the first case (wherein it appears that I bought it in order to murder people at the market) is different from "I bought a machine gun" in the second case (wherein my intention is not apparent). When we say, "Linda is a bank teller," we understand her to currently do the work of bank tellers. She is, therefore, part of the set of currently active bank tellers. When we say, however, "Linda is a bank teller who is active in the feminist movement," we may infer that she was trained as a bank teller or that she once worked as a bank teller, in addition to the possibility that she is currently doing the work of a bank teller. In this interpretation, the experiment reveals that people may not use the rules of first-order logic in order to parse natural language sentences—hardly a surprise to cognitive linguists and philosophers who have figured out that logical form and grammatical structure are different (Hacking, 1984; Lakoff & Johnson, 1999).

An Interpersonal Interpretation   H. P. Grice (1975) proposed that conversations between people cannot be understood simply by reference to the transcript of their conversation and to a dictionary or thesaurus that translates words and phrases and parses grammatical structures. Rather, the meaning that one gives to a phrase uttered in a conversation depends on one's assumptions about the intentions of the person uttering the sentence, which are themselves related in many ways to the immediate context of the sentence. Grice proposed that people assume each other to be cooperative and therefore try to interpret each other's words so as to make them informative and relevant to a particular topic. If one assumes that the laws of probability are a priori dispositive of the choice between the statements "Linda is a bank teller" and "Linda is a bank teller who is active in the feminist movement" as to their relative likelihood, then one must infer that the description of Linda in the experimental materials is irrelevant. But this contradicts Grice's cooperation principle. In order to find it relevant, one must find an interpretation of the problem (and we have shown that there are several available) which allows one to consider all of the information given by the experimenter as relevant and informative. Choosing "Linda is a bank teller who is active in the feminist movement" as more likely to be true than "Linda is a bank teller" is no more than a signal that the participant was trying to solve an interpersonal problem vis à vis the experimenter rather than the first-order problem which he or she was apparently resolving. The work of Norbert Schwarz and his coworkers (Schwarz, Strack, & Mai, 1991; Schwarz & Bless, 1992; Schwarz, 1988) suggests an explanation for representativeness-based judgments that is similar to the Gricean logic in its emphasis on the information imparted to a person by the context of the conversation. The representativeness heuristic (Tversky & Kahneman, 1982) relates to the propensity of people to make judgments about the likelihood of the validity of a universal proposition ("My life is going well") on the basis of statements about particular circumstances that are deemed to be "representative" of the reference class of the universal proposition ("my marriage is going well"). In the experiment run by Schwarz, Strack, and Mai (1991), people from one group were first asked how satisfied they were with their lives in general and then asked how satisfied they were with their marital situations. The researchers found a correlation coefficient of 0.32 between the (coded) answers to the two questions. In a second group, the order of the questions was reversed, and the correlation coefficient increased to 0.67 (Schwarz, Strack, & Mai, 1991). Schwarz (1988) offers a purely cognitive explanation for the effect: "Presumably, answering the marital satisfaction question first rendered information about one's marriage highly accessible and this, rather than other, information, was subsequently used in evaluating one's life as a whole" (Schwarz, 1988). In the Linda example, what is prima facie accessible is the congruence between the description of Linda and the suggestion that she is active in the feminist movement; and by the explanation offered by Schwarz, it is the accessibility of some decision rule, rather than the presumed intent of the speaker, that accounts for the conjunction bias.

Not all of these explanations can be used to synthesize alternative normative models of judgment formation under uncertainty, but some can; yet they have not been brought into the mainstream study of managerial thinking *because* they were never in the mainstream of psychological thinking. What does psychology make—for instance—of Charlie Munger's very precise articulation of a worldly wisdom based on a negative heuristic of testing and selection of ideas that has far less in common with any Bayesian-probabilistic-inductivist approach to belief than it does with a sophisticated form of falsificationism? Even a superficial approach to epistemological tradition that minimally attempts to cover more than one approach to valid inference from empirical "fact" reveals that several normative models of epistemic rationality coexist in vigorous and seemingly irresolvable debate. For example:

1. Falsificationism and Probabilism (Gemes, 1997). Whereas probabilists believe that degrees of belief satisfying the laws of the probability calculus can and should be used as "measures" of credence (for subjectivists) or truth (for objectivists) (Howson, 2001), falsificationists (Popper, 1959; elaborated in Gemes, 1997, which makes a pedagogical *excursus* on the subject) argue *from the premises of probabilism* itself that the probability of any law-like universal statement is identically zero and therefore that the probabilistic approach to belief formation is uninformative (and therefore irrational). In exchange, Popper (1973) offers up a "measure of verisimilitude" of a *theory* (not just of a single belief) which is an increasing function of the unrefuted empirical content of the theory in question.

2. *Various Forms of Falsificationism* (Lakatos, 1970; Popper, 1973; Miller, 1974, as cited in Miller, 1994; Niilinuto, 1998). Miller (1974; as cited in Miller, 1994), however, showed that Popper's verisimilitude measure is invalid (and his argument was accepted by Popper, 1999). In the meantime, however, Lakatos (1970) proposed an elaboration of falsificationism that distinguished between dogmatic falsificationism (accepting evidence statements unquestioningly) and methodological falsificationism (subjecting evidence statements to empirical critiques similar to those directed at theories, aiming to uncover the theories embedded in the evidence statements and prescribing critical empirical tests of *these* theories) and between naïve methodological falsificationism (more or less automatically applying the falsificationist ethic to theories and evidence statements without regard to a theory choice required for action) and sophisticated methodological falsificationism (stipulating criteria for theory choice after repeated empirical testing and reflection). Popper (1973), however, did not accept Lakatos's (1970) elaboration of falsificationism, and several strands of falsificationism have continued to coexist.

3. *Various Forms of Probabilism (Howson, 1995).* Probabilism is also *M*-furcated. Probabilities can be "objectively" interpreted as limiting frequencies (von Mises, 1939), as reflections of the mathematical odds of an event (Laplace, 1799), as subjective degrees of belief (Bayes, 1763), or as *propensities* of entities to behave in particular ways on particular occasions (Popper, 1983); and this list is not exhaustive (see Howson, 1995). The requirement that probabilities (in whatever form) obey the axioms of probability theory is not necessarily one that follows from a "more fundamental" axiom of individual rationality (Howson, 2001). A classic argument for why one's degrees of belief should obey the axioms of the probability calculus (and that therefore no "normative" belief producer should, for instance, commit the "conjunction fallacy") is that, if one does not obey these axioms, a third party could construct a "Dutch book" against the believer in question—a collection of bets that, if taken, would cause the latter to lose money *for sure* (De Finetti, 1937). Whether or not it is *rational* to measure one's beliefs in ways that exposes one to Dutch books, however, is dependent on the antecedent plausibility of the claim that someone is, in fact, willing and able to create such a book (Moldoveanu & Langer, 2002). This observation suggests a new approach to *teaching* probabilistic reasoning in the MBA classroom—as a prudential logic for making public bets rather than as jack-of-all-trades logic of thought—which we take up in detail in chapter 3.

4. Various Shortcomings of Probabilism and Their Repairs. It is not clear—as a foundational point—that we have a unique and satisfactory answer to the following question: Are numerical decision weights or degree of belief (belief measures) sufficiently rich representations for the phenomena they aim to capture, or do we need to augment our representational space altogether? Let us illustrate: Heath and Tversky (1991) asked participants in their studies to provide subjective degrees of belief for an event drawn from a class in which participants thought themselves expert or at least cognizant (such as the outcome of a football game for football fans) and also for an event drawn from a class in which participants most likely considered themselves ignorant (the probability of precipitation in Sydney, Australia, on a particular summer day, for instance). They then asked participants to choose between betting on the event for which they supplied subjective probabilities and betting on an "objective" lottery with probability of winning equal to the subjective probability measure. They observed that participants were more likely to bet on a familiar event than on a lottery with probability of winning equal to their subjective degree of belief about the occurrence of that event but that they exhibited the opposite preference in the case of unfamiliar events. Whatever else this result indicates, it suggests that probability measures do not fully capture the epistemic state of the choosing participant, as there *is* something different among lotteries defined on familiar events and lotteries defined on unfamiliar events, but this difference will not be picked up by looking at the probability measure alone. Faced with this ambiguity, we may try to "repair" the probability calculus by referring to higher order probabilities (degrees of belief about the degrees of belief one has produced), by introducing a multidimensional representation of beliefs (which contains not only their "strength" but also information about their source), or by attempting a new representation of beliefs altogether. Each one of these approaches is likely to lead to different views of cognitive rationality and to different research programs, depending on the kind of "warrant" that we will admit as a backer for a probabilistic statement and the admissible form that this warrant may take.

5. Various Shortcomings of Computationalism and Their Ameliorations. Normative models of decision making currently used have a common *algorithmic* structure: they can be represented as algorithms running on computational hardware structures. As such, they instantiate a broader commitment to the "mind-as-computer" metaphor that has colored much theorizing and experimental work in cognitive psychology for the past 50 years (Gigerenzer & Goldstein, 1996). More recently, researchers have focused on less-well-structured representations of internal psychological processes that can be used to capture decision making in "real world" settings, such as metaphors, analogies, scripts, and narratives (Klein, 1998). Although such representations seem to lead to decision making that "works"—relative to the decision maker's standards, as well as to objective standards of "success" in particular settings—very little analytical work has been done in understanding and comparing various metaphors, analogies, and narrative structures with regard to their long-run success and generalizability from localized field situations.

Thus, in matters of cognition and cognitive rationality, we find ourselves in the presence of a burgeoning theoretical pluralism. Healthy, vigorous debate—rather than subdued deference to a clearly superior model—is what should *and could* characterize the field as a whole. There is no clear argument against broadening the spectrum of models of epistemic rationality that the field should consider, and there is significant opportunity for advancing the depth and accuracy of our understanding of decision making by broadening the class of a priori models and representations that researchers bring to their studies. We turn next to a model of how such an expansion could be accomplished.

Loosening the Straitjacket: New and "Clashing" Models for the Study of Managerial Judgments

If we are not a priori justified in assuming that the narrow region of *justificationism–probabilism–Bayesianism* is where we should concentrate our search for normative lenses for managerial cognition, then it makes sense to look comparatively at other epistemological stances as possible candidates for normative lenses for the systematic study of the ways in which managers form and update beliefs. The literature offers few examples of studies of managerial cognition that begin from noninductivist, non-Bayesian cognitive models. Chris Argyris's work (see, for instance, the essays in (Argyris, 1993a) as an illustrative example) does stress (albeit implicitly) a falsificationist approach to belief validation. However, his work makes no attempt to systematically characterize and "map" managerial cognition in a way that is analogous to that undertaken by proponents of the "heuristics and biases" research program—as a set of systematic departures from the falsificationist epistemology Argyris endorses. Because it is not based (yet) on a clearly defined (and formalizable) model of epistemic rationality, it cannot render precise measures of departures from such rationality; but this is an *opportunity* for new work, and certainly not a sound reason against developing the falsificationist perspective into an empirical program in its own right.

Gary Klein's studies of naturalistic decision making (Klein, 1998) attempts to break out of the representational straitjackets of *both* classical Bayesian decision analysis *and* algorithmically tractable representations of decision making, but his work culminates in a mere *taxonomy* of new representational concepts for studying decision making in naturalistic settings, which could gain prescriptive force from a systematic dialogue with the a priori models of classical epistemology; such a dialogue could come to tell us *why* and *how* such "unconventional" approaches to decision making work, not only *that* they work.

Broadening the spectrum of a priori models that we use to study managerial and organizational decision making involves (1) a significant investment in understanding the normative foundations for alternative models and (2) a significant investment in *interpreting* decision streams exhibited by managers in different types of organizations in light of newly introduced cognitive strategies.

As Moldoveanu and Singh (2003) point out, there *is* reason to believe that the kinds of cognitive strategies and schemata represented by sophisticated methodological falsificationism are functionally more useful to practicing managers than are strategies based on inductive and probabilistic reasoning, in spite of the fact that the probability calculus does provide a persuasive logic for laying public bets. If the dynamics of business models and ideas can be validly represented by an *evolutionary logic* of variation, selection, and retention, and if selection can be understood as a form of refutation (the nonsurvival of the unfit), then an evolutionary approach to belief validation (which a sophisticated methodological falsificationist approach surely is) can be understood as an internal simulation of external evolutionary processes; that is, as a form of *virtual evolution* that provides the model checklist that Munger seeks but does not find in formalized education (Munger, 1997).

Managerial thinking that follows such an approach performs low-stakes, in vitro experimental tests of ideas that would otherwise have had to have been submitted to much higher stakes tests in the "real world." Because a mind that is capable of performing a competent simulation of a phenomenon is more likely to generate valid predictions of that phenomenon than a mind that does not have this capability, the argument provides a reason for believing that falsificationist approaches would dominate justificationist (including inductivist) approaches in the "real world" of high-stakes business organizations (which may itself select for falsificationists). Thus we have grounds for branching out in our study of managerial cognition and to absorb questions of epistemic rationality *into* the field of study (rather than solving them in other fields and importing the results into the study of managerial cognition). Of course, a purely a priori analysis of *any* phenomenon may be completely misguided: the normative schema used to "understand" the phenomenon may be completely dysfunctional. "Field epistemology" rises to this challenge by putting the researcher in a position to "learn from the subject," thus forgoing monopoly on "the correct way of forming and validating beliefs" and retreating to the more modest claim of merely providing a structured language in which findings from the field can be appropriated.

The key benefit of such a language over the narrow Bayesian tool kit is that it is at once broader but no less analytically "clean." Various forms of falsificationism *can* be articulated with the same analytical precision with which Bayesian decision-making axioms have been (Lakatos, 1970; Gemes, 1997) and can be defended against probabilist attacks with the same persuasiveness with which probabilism can be defended against falsificationist challenges (Gemes, 1997). Far from being a discouraging factor, the lack of definite resolution in matters epistemological should be considered a positive factor, an invitation to develop contingency theories of cognitive rationality and to develop models that heed the experience of successful practitioners who regularly inquire into the unknown and come out of the process alive or thriving.

What would a research agenda for new "field epistemology" look like? Here is a proposal.

Renewing the Methodological Debate to Bring Different Epistemological Stances to Life

Breathing life into a new research program based on a broadened set of a priori models is dependent on renewing debate within the field about what a successful epistemological stance consists of. In turn, the substance and depth of such a debate depends critically on broadening the class of candidate models that are considered. Epistemological analysis consists precisely of giving reasons and counterreasons for the ecological validity of various ways of probing into the unknown—of producing beliefs and belief validation strategies that satisfy the requirements of accuracy, truth, objectivity, and internal and external validity that adequate belief validation mechanisms must satisfy. Naturalistic decision-making studies can contribute to this debate a set of criteria and decision conditions (time constraints, ill-definedness of decision goals (Klein, 1998)) that can broaden the traditional standards of success that have been considered definitive by epistemologists whose reasoning is not informed by intelligent practice.

Studying Epistemological Stances Comparatively
Using Analytical and Computational Methods

Alternative epistemological stances can be compared on the basis of analysis and computational simulations. The question, What constitutes a successful learning strategy? can be examined computationally by simulating naturalistic decision scenarios and measuring the performance of various learning algorithms with respect to their accuracy (goodness of fit, minimization of variance), generalizability (simplicity, invariance with respect to a wide range of conditions of decision-making settings) and rate of convergence to an acceptable answer (measuring their relative performance in time-constrained decision situations).

Studying Epistemological Stances Comparatively
Using Experimental Methods

The pervasive underdetermination of theory by evidence statements poses a deep problem for the experimental researcher in matters epistemological, as our previous examples illustrate. The "Linda" experiment carried out by Kahneman and Tversky and held to illustrate the "conjunction fallacy" can be interpreted in many different ways, depending on prior theoretical commitments. This does not mean, however, that it is impossible to perform decisive and penetrating experimental analysis of styles of reasoning and decision making on a broadened map of a priori models: experiments can and should be designed to distinguish not only among "normative" and "nonnormative" decision makers vis-à-vis a standard model of rationality, but also among decision makers who conform to different models of rationality. Thereafter, the success of different learning and decision-making strategies can be tested by having subjects who conform to different epistemological stances compete head-to-head in weakly structured decision-making tasks.

Studying Epistemological Stances
Using Empirical Methods

Perhaps more important, epistemological analysis and a broadened map of possible epistemological stances can be used to inform field studies of managers and organizations exploring and prospecting their opportunity sets, as our previous examples illustrate. In these cases, a broadened class of a priori models can be understood as supplying a structured language for understanding successful and unsuccessful patterns of empirical reasoning, for explaining why certain styles work better than others in the field.

Of course, epistemological analysis alone cannot be the sole arbiter of cognitive rationality, as criteria for high-quality decision making vary with the context of the decision. Practitioners themselves can be usefully regarded as innovators in matters epistemological; they may, in fact, be, all things considered, *more* cognitively rational than researchers who study them using restricted sets of models of judgment and decision making. In this case, a broadened epistemological map provides a language in which *we can represent what we have learned from the subject:* a structured set of decision algorithms and representations in which epistemic innovation from the field can be conceptualized and reentered into the epistemological debate.

This brings to a close our discussion of the pragmatics of loosening disciplinary straitjackets in one particular field, a discussion that is meant as an invitation to broaden and extend the analysis to other fields as well. Indeed, the epistemological and ontic commitments of various approaches to human relations, strategic planning, and design and organizational analysis await exploration and unpacking, to the end of producing new research agendas that take full advantage of the diversity and plurality that lies within them and that will be energized by an awareness of this inner variety.

3

Business School 3.0

The Design and Development of Integrative "Cognitive-Behavioral Modules" for the Thinker of the Future

Learning how... *is not like learning* that, *or acquiring information.*
Truths can be imparted, procedures can only be inculcated.
Gilbert Ryle, The Concept of Mind

The fundamental building blocks for designing the high-value decision maker of the future exist today on the premises of business schools worldwide. However, designing the program that puts these building blocks together is a difficult and delicate enterprise. Here is why:

1. Even though business schools are *already* multidisciplinary (they are aggregates of representatives of many disciplines) and sometimes pluridisciplinary (they are *aware* of being multidisciplinary) collectives, they are not yet *inter*disciplinary (they do not cross disciplinary boundaries in ways that do justice to all of the bridged disciplines and successfully integrate across boundaries) or transdisciplinary ones. The limiting function of communication codes common to some disciplines but not others and idiosyncratic institutional practices of various disciplines make the coordinated delivery of complex, mixed, or heterogeneous conceptual structures costly. To see what is at issue, consider the difficulties faced by one who would like to replace teaching by materials, such as case studies, tailored to theories familiar to the instructor with teaching by the use of complex historical narratives that are analyzed in each class according to several different, diligently and rigorously pursued theoretical perspectives: detailed biographical accounts of line managers, for instance, can be analyzed using several different models of human behavior drawn from economics, neuropsychology, and different psychoanalytical approaches. The difficulty lies as much in bringing about the change in the "raw material" (from tailored case studies to untailored narratives), which is bound to increase

the complexity of the classroom experience in ways that run counter to students' expectations, as in inducing cooperation among instructors on the complicated task of a coordinated delivery that has uncertain individual benefits, unpredictable marginal costs, and high fixed costs.

2. The microincentives of untenured and tenured academics alike make cross-disciplinary collaboration on either teaching or research difficult to mandate and even more difficult to plan. Indeed, the "success stories" of interdisciplinary innovation (behavioral economics, for instance) have been unplanned activity sets, linked together by cleverly constructed *ex post* narratives. Daniel Kahneman and Amos Tversky, for instance, did not plan to set up an interdisciplinary communicative field composed of psychologists, economists, and analytical philosophers concerned with the study of human judgments and decisions but merely to provide an experimentally motivated critique of the axiomatic foundations of rational-choice theory and microeconomics. Ronald Coase, similarly, did not set out to create a subfield of organization theory concerned with the parsimonious analysis of modes of organizing work and exchange as a function of production and transactions costs but rather to provide an uncertainty-reduction-driven foundation for the analysis of firm boundaries.

3. The spectatorial and gladiatorial structure of the interaction between instructor and students in the MBA classroom setting makes the pursuit of authentic dialogue aimed at unpacking assumptions, opening avenues for exploration, and raising questions difficult. Rather, the emphasis often remains on achieving some kind of "legitimate closure" to the interaction, one that preserves the epistemic authority of the instructor (see, for instance, Argyris, 1980, for an illuminating exposition of the dynamic in the context of executive education settings).

4. The cognitive and representational dimension of knowledge that is often emphasized and understood as that which is being transferred from instructor to student in the classroom inhibits a full appreciation of the full *performative* dimension of business knowledge—of the causal import to the self, for instance, of adopting a particular model of the self and living with and within that model as a regulative framework. MBA talk is often "idle" talk, as Mintzberg has argued (Mintzberg, 2004); even when the dramaturgical and strategic dimensions of his speech acts do not take over the real classroom speaker and lead him or her in directions that run counter to communication-focused dialogue, the interaction that emerges remains at the level of "just so" stories and arguments. The question of how to get "skin in the game" from the participants remains open, and the problem of turning academic understanding into embodied

understanding (the intelligent production of behavior) remains unaddressed. The question is at the heart of the difference between the *ontic* and *ontological* dimensions discussed previously. In particular, for a set of concepts and categories to escape the purely ontic realm (of merely cognitive understanding and categorization), in which much of academic discourse lives, and become *ontologies* that guide and shape managerial action, classroom behavior must be produced that embodies them and thus makes them real. Knowing the set of logically compatible rules one might use to set up a competitive game interaction between firms or individuals, for instance (the *ontic* realm), is different from actually using a competitive game model to structure one's interactions with a spouse, coworker, or competitor, which takes seeing the other as a competing player and the interaction as a zero-sum game, iteratively eliminating the dominated strategies and acting on the logical implications of this conceptualization and resulting model to produce effects that are causally linked to one's model of the interaction. Chris Argyris's repeated challenge to social scientists (tightly encapsulated in the adage "If you think you understand a particular behavior, then *produce it*") can be understood as a recognition of the gap between the ontic and the ontological dimensions of knowledge and of the overwhelming importance of the ontological dimension to the enterprises of education and development.

4. The *student-as-consumer* model (Pfeffer & Fong, 2002, 2004; Mintzberg, 2004), coupled with the *knowledge-as-food* (or "valuable material stuff") metaphor (underlying the demand of students for "takeaways") for the outcome of the classroom experience—which could include the classroom experience itself, as in various forms of *info*tainment and *edu*tainment—makes it costly for any single instructor to single-handedly undertake changes that violate a zone of security for the participants or for other instructors. As with any program of training based on sleep- and vital-resource deprivation (the prototypical first year of the MBA program), relatively complex stimuli without immediate meaning or usefulness and reward-and-punishment regimes that look quasi random to the participants (largely due to the mismatch between assignment writers and assignment graders, which in turn can be traced to the "mass production" approach to producing MBAs), features such as simplicity of stimulus and immediacy and predictability of reward come to be craved, prized, and rewarded by the trainees above other potential sources of value. The potential for creating an environment in which concepts are turned into ontologies and theories into action maps is often lost as a result, as these processes are risky undertakings that on both interpersonal and intrapersonal levels require an availability of presence

and tolerance for risk and ambiguity that is lost as a result of the emotional landscape of the training process.

These problems can be addressed through the adoption of a new way of looking at the MBA experience, one that does not do violence to the current disciplinary and conceptual base of business academia but rather uses this base to produce a new kind of educational experience, which we refer to as a "practicum."

The Practicum: A Structural Solution Concept for the MBA of the Future

A practicum is an interactive experience for students and educators that unveils and brings to the fore the often hidden epistemological, ontic, ontological, and performative dimensions of the knowledge imparted in the MBA classroom (figure 3.1). It takes advantage of, rather than

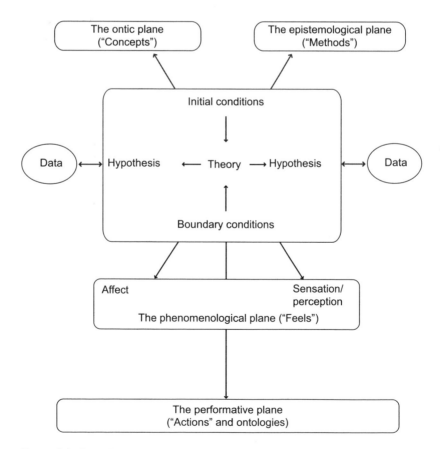

Figure 3.1. Basic Dimensions of Business Knowledge

suppressing or attempting to do away with, the fundamental tensions and problems that are implicit in the often theatrical experience of the classroom—such as the suppression of sharp dissent or radical difference, the unidimensional authority structure of discourse, and the monoparadigmatic approach to validating knowledge, of which students are to greater or lesser degrees aware—and uses these tensions to produce experiences that cultivate not only erudition, knowledge of the "codes of business," and the competent use of buzz words and frameworks but also functionally useful cognitive-behavioral modules that begin to address the gap between the skills currently trained and the skills of the integrator—the high-value decision maker of the future.

The form of the practicum is patterned on the musical master class, the psychotherapeutic training session, and the design practicum introduced by the Bauhaus school. In the musical master class, the student attempts to come to a better, deeper—but always embodied—understanding of the score and of his or her own performative capabilities with regard to the score. The function of the instructor is to guide the process of forming and shaping this understanding, offering suggestions for improvement and criticisms but leaving ultimate decision rights and the assumption of implementation risks in the hands of the student. The format of the musical master class makes mere theoretical argument and presentation *by itself* moot. No matter how articulate he or she is at adducing arguments about the score, the performer must ultimately *produce* behavior that exemplifies these theories in order to make a real contribution to the class as a whole: the all-important schism between theory and practice that renders classical education causally impotent to produce lasting behavioral change is eliminated.

The psychotherapeutic training session allows the trainee the latitude to experiment with different modes of being relative to a situation in which she or he has a complex goal admitting of many possible interpretations—essentially facing a wicked problem of the type we discussed in chapter 1—and gives her or him the benefit of feedback about the products, processes, and procedures that she or he designs and enacts. The training session creates an environment in which behavior must not only be *produced* but also *tried and tested,* and the results of the experiments must be interpreted in real time; thus it essentially replicates the predicament of the action scientist (Argyris & Schon, 1978) who faces the unknown armed with a battery of personal technologies of inquiry and interpretation that allow him or her to "ask rather than guess" and to change behavior in response to new information.

The Bauhaus design curriculum is based on the mechanical development of basic and relevant skill sets (freehand drawing, sculpting, painting, technical drawing, two- and three-dimensional drawing, computer-aided design of complex surfaces) that are brought together every year into projects that require participants to make use of the skills developed during a particular term or year. The Bauhaus curriculum is based at once on the realization that the designer's critical skills are *tacit*—hence they are developed by *doing*—and on the realization that the designer's task is an integrator's task—one of essentially *making objects* by the intelligent deployment of skill sets that live in the tacit dimension.

The practicum-oriented curriculum recognizes that the integrator's integration-related skills are largely tacit; hence the need for a project as an integrative exercise, in contrast to a series of lectures that merely provide psychological or psychoanalytic accounts of successful artists and designers whose creations exemplify particular integration techniques. The emphasis on the embodiment of mechanically developed skills in design-oriented projects also addresses the usual incentive problem of asking students to develop capabilities—which requires work that may be tedious—without giving them a proximal incentive to use these skills in a way that makes them theirs. In lecture- and exam-based classes, exams often come to measure how well one does on exams, which only infrequently proxies for what one really likes to know, which is how well the skill set required to solve certain kinds of problems has been articulated. This approach recognizes that skills are very peculiar sets of "objects" in that they are always already entwined with the purpose to which they are used; they are *skills-for-achieving-X* as much as they are *skills-for-doing-Y*; and the project supplies a proximal, tangible, motivating X that can be designed to induce the desired Y.

Although the *form* of the practicum is new to the MBA culture, the cognitive-behavioral modules that make it up are not new to business school scholars, who always already *are* modelers of human behavior, experimenters, epistemologists, and conceptual innovators and—although less frequently—*producers* of organizational effects. For this reason, the practicum concept promises to *dissolve* the tension between the need for a radically new approach to MBA education that trains the tacit skills we have called out and the current endowment, resource base, and culture of business academia and scholarship: it takes advantage of the promising trends that we have identified in business academia and efficiently uses them to a new pedagogical purpose.

The basic idea behind the practicum is simple. As we argued, what business academics *do* when they write down and refine models of human and organizational behavior, validate these models, communicate with one another across boundaries and schisms between different ways of seeing, modeling, representing, and knowing in ways meant to advance various individual and institutional aims constitutes a set of skills that are uniquely valuable to the high-value decision maker of the future and, we argue, significantly more valuable than the acquisition of declarative information and knowledge structures that are putatively "about business." Given that the half-life of papers in the field is 2.5 to 5 years, it is not remarkable that the value of "know-what" in business academia is under attack from many different perspectives (Bennis & O'Toole, 2004; Mintzberg, 2004); what is remarkable is the value that, we argue, is to be found in the know-how currently residing in business schools.

There are two models for understanding and deploying the practicum in the context of an educational program such as the MBA once its core components have been articulated. The first (the "thought-and-behavior design and experimentation lab") relies on the development of these modules in small laboratory-like settings with low student-to-faculty ratios that enable the creation of a personalized space for understanding, producing, and trying out thinking and behavior. This model is based on attracting existing or new faculty members to the project of creating a focused training environment aimed at developing skills that can be deployed by their beholders to the conventional settings of the MBA classroom and to other domains of their lives.

The second model (the "communicative space design" model) relies on the attempt to develop valuable cognitive-behavioral modules as an *integral part* of the educational curriculum. Because the modules and the skills they embody are *know-how*, rather than *know-what*, in nature, they are compatible with many possible declarative knowledge structures and problem statements—and therefore with many different substantive agendas. One can train, for instance, a disciplined falsificationist in strategy, marketing, or organizational behavior classes and contexts, and one can cultivate a trainee's capabilities for communicating across incommensurable hermeneutic circles within the space of problems that a human resources specialist faces or within the universe of problems that a technical program manager faces.

Model I. The Thought-and-Behavior Design and Experimentation Lab

Module 1. Articulation: The Adaptive Generation of Models and Representations

The first module aims to teach trainees to become creators and developers of models of human and organizational behavior, to train model makers and model shapers rather than model takers. This is one of the fundamental crafts of the social scientist, who creates representations of people and organizations either out of basic explanatory logics, such as rational-choice and rational-belief axioms, interactive epistemology ("game theory"), evolutionary schemata based on the logic of variation, selection, and retention, learning and adaptation schemata based on selective reinforcement and selective validation, diffusion schemata and representations of the evolution and dynamics of rule-based systems (cellular automata models, including $NK(C)$ models of coevolutionary processes and dynamical network models) or—far less frequently—through the creation of new building blocks and the refinement and modification of the basic building blocks inherited from mainstream social science.

Together, these modeling building blocks can be understood as a *library of forms*—a basic repertoire of cognitive productions (in the language of Simon, 1990) or a set of "nuts and bolts for social scientists" (in the language of Elster, 1982) that can be deployed to build detailed models of individual and social phenomena by mapping theoretical constructs to intersubjectively agreeable observation statements, defining constitutive, causal, and other-than-causal relationships between them, articulating a set of assumptions about initial and boundary conditions for the applicability of the resulting model, and then producing explanations that use one or more modes of explanation—causal, functional, or intentional (Elster, 1982). Trainees are introduced to model building as an activity—a *praxis*—as a way of articulating and solving problems that do not come prepackaged in a disciplinary language and as a way of unpacking and analyzing narratives and of understanding others' representations at a level of specificity that allows disagreements to be sharply formulated.

Lay language is always already metaphorical in nature and thus embedded in mental models that can be expected to be shared by many individuals without formalized training (Lakoff & Johnson, 1999): *time is money, good is up and bad is down, the self is a container, the brain is a machine,* and *the mind represents a sequence of states of that machine* are—as Lakoff and Johnson show—not just mere sayings that we utter without any special commitment, intention, or effect; rather, they shape and structure both the ways in which we think about time, morality, and ourselves, brains, and minds *and* the universe of conceivable actions that we think we can take around these objects. Mere ways of speaking become ontologies in everyday praxis. The articulation module faces the challenge of getting trainees to conceptualize the models that are already embedded in the way they speak and think, of understanding the ways in which concepts shape behavior, and—where suitable—changing their core representations using the generative semantics of social science models, a process that often takes place unconsciously as a result of prolonged training in one of the basic social sciences. On this background, the classroom encounter can be understood as a meeting of the trainee with a set of concepts—the modeler's tool kit—that have been refined through a web of disciplined communicative interactions—the "academic project"—and have become candidates themselves for becoming ontologies through the understanding and actions of trainees who understand and appropriate them.

Consider these examples:

1. An unreflective view of the concept "self" that has some *actual* selves (other people) represented as causal automatons and other actual selves ("me") represented as either causal automatons ("I was forced to...") or as beings capable of free will ("I chose to..."), depending on the microincentives of the situation, can be made explicit and brought into contact with other conceptions of self prevalent in some disciplines (a set of preferences and logical constraints and a dynamic maximization function) that can be applied in a self-consistent fashion across many different selves (mine and other selves) to generate an integrative model of human interactions.

2. A "lay" conception of probability that functions as a catchall for (variously) a set of frequencies, the inverse of the number of independent possible outcomes, and a "gut feeling" that cannot be attached by the mind of the trainee to any fact about the world which he or she can get someone else to agree with can be brought to the light of explicit understanding and contrasted with different conceptions of probability that can be compared with one another with respect to both epistemic and pragmatic virtues and narrowed down to a concept that can be self-consistently applied across different situations.

Because "mental models are everywhere," because they come in many incommensurable shapes and sizes, and precisely because they are causally powerful, an articulation module aimed at uncovering the cognitive structure of everyday managerial life and sharpening the mental representations that trainees use in making sense of their own lives can be a powerful intervention, one that social scientists are in a good position to pursue given their own engagement with the task and process of modeling.

Module 2. Validation: The Selective Retention of Useful Mental Objects and the Analysis of Subterfuge

The second module attempts to develop and cultivate applied falsificationists and sophisticated experimentalists. To the trained social scientist, the world often appears as an experimental playground—as a sequence of actual or possible experiments designed to test interesting hypotheses (Abelson, Frey & Gregg, 2004; Langer, personal communication, 2000). The cognitive "scaffolding"—as well as the affective anchor—of the scientist's beliefs is (ideally) responsive to the results of experiments carried out with the aim of refuting the hypotheses that follow from these beliefs and biased in favor of belief sets that can, in practice and not only in theory, be empirically tested. What makes the results of scientific experiments intriguing and worthwhile understanding is precisely the "danger" in which the experimenter has placed his or her own hypotheses in the experiment (Popper, 1959; Lakatos, 1970). Thus the activities of intellectually honest, disciplined scientists instantiate skill sets that closely resemble those of the tough-minded integrator, which we do not usually expect to find in the lay person. Indeed, if for the lay person "beliefs are like possessions" (Abelson, 1986), whereas for the falsificationist epistemologist and scientist they are more like "walking sticks" (Roethlisberger, 1980) or trial balloons, then one can expect significant gains from an interaction in which not only the idea of falsificationism but also its basic emotional and behavioral correlates are transferred to trainees.

The module aims to develop both the cognitive and the affective and behavioral correlates of the empirically minded falsificationist by getting trainees to understand the often counterproductive—self-sealing and self-justifying—architectures of belief that they cultivate and practice in "everyday" settings (because they "feel good") and then introducing the often counterintuitive logic of falsification, which distinguishes sharply between testable and nontestable beliefs and favors the former over the latter, emphasizes the role of deductive logic in connecting beliefs with evidence statements that corroborate or disconfirm them, exposes the fallibility of evidence statements—which can themselves be criticized through empirical tests of the theories embedded in them—and highlights the role of conscious but provisional decisions in the selection of one theory over others as a basis for action. The falsificationist logic can then be applied to reengineer the belief networks that trainees provide (in the form of their own beliefs and the reasons for them) and to create refutation-oriented tests—often in the form of experiments and quasi experiments—which can be used to subject the original beliefs to empirical tests. The approach uses as raw input belief networks generated by participants themselves. The "emotional temperature" of the exercise can be increased or decreased according to the belief classes that one elicits: *weakly held, closely held, indispensable* (beliefs) is one possible typology that permits investigation of the effects of reengineering belief sets in different regimes of affective attachment to one's beliefs.

The falsificationist logic can be understood as a basis for Chris Argyris's approach to reengineering counterproductive interpersonal communication patterns. As Argyris points out (Argyris, 1993a), self-sealing, self-justifying, and self-reinforcing approaches to communication inhibit learning by blocking the paths by which individuals can question each others' assumptions, unspoken beliefs about one another, and intentions and lead interlocutors to create large-scale, untestable, and mal-adaptive interpersonal belief networks that in turn lead to the compulsive repetition of counterproductive interpersonal behaviors. The falsificationist mind-set can be used as an intervention tool for the reengineering of such interpersonal patterns. Just as falsificationism requires asserting, arguing to support the assertion, specifying the conditions under which the assertion would be false, and then testing, learning-oriented communication combines *advocacy* corresponding to hypothesis formulation and argumentation—with *inquiry* (Argyris, 1993a), corresponding to hypothesis testing through empirical experimentation. Thus, "difficult interactions" and "tough conversation" can be turned into experimental fields for the development of a valuable skill—through the reengineering approach introduced earlier. The module's success depends on its designer's ability to confound the artificial boundary between "science" and "life" by abstracting from science the essential cognitive and emotional landscape that can turn a mere conversation into a sequence of maximally informative experiments.

*Module 3. Communication: The Ethics of Discourse
and the Public Practice of Reason*

Academia can function as a powerful theory- and model-validation engine just to the extent that the communication community that it constitutes is governed by a discourse ethics aimed at mitigating the number of *self-defeating communicative acts*. Self-defeating communicative acts are acts that undermine or negate the role of their producer as a member of the communication community (Apel, 1980; Habermas, 1987). Refusing to answer a question about one's assumptions, for instance, is self-defeating because it is akin to a withdrawal from the dialogue or discussion and therefore akin to saying *I am not part of this conversation*, a statement that relies, for intelligibility as a speech act, on the very act of participation that it explicitly denies. Lying is a self-defeating speech act because it is a negation of the implicit commitment of each communicator to say things that are truthful (Habermas, 1987). Producing (nonverbal) passive-aggressive behavior and refusing to answer calls to account for it is a self-defeating communicative act because it negates the implicit commitment of the communicator to say things that are truth-like. In looking out for logical inconsistencies, for semantic confusion and ambiguity (one word used in more than one way in the same text), for logically relevant but unexamined assumptions, for independent or incommensurable arguments purporting to be logically connected, academic reviewers instantiate—and submit to—a(often implicit) discourse ethics. Indeed, most would acknowledge the aim of eliminating self-defeating communicative acts from their communication community (even though few realize just how far reaching such a commitment is).

Although discourse ethics has been criticized as a general ethical principle because it does not guarantee convergence to an agreement which it in fact aims to produce, its use as a powerful *integration tool* has not been signaled to date. Because its assumptions are relatively unobjection-able and the commitments it secures from participants to a conversation are very far reaching (Moldoveanu, 2000) and include a commitment to (deductive) logical coherence and inclusiveness of potentially radically different points of view—discourse ethics *is* an integrative interpersonal technology. It secures a common and legitimate foundation for inquiry aimed at unpacking the assumptions and understanding the worldviews of the *others* that would otherwise have to rest on idiosyncratic prefer-ences and values (such as a value for curiosity or an idiosyncratic value for tough-mindedness).

A communicative module will aim to transfer the often implicit dis-course ethics of the academic review and debate setting to the trainee by instantiating interactions in which self-defeating communicative acts are sanctioned, for instance, through penalties to credibility and public recognition. The module makes no special demands on the substantive context of the interaction—the topic of the conversation—but challenges explicitly the "standard procedures" by which MBA instructors drive dis-cussions "to closure," for the very standards that are assumed to be dis-positive of a particular claim will now be questionable and criticizable. "*I'll show you the data*" (for a particular hypothesis that does not accord with a student's intuition), for instance, cannot function as a self-evident "clincher" of a classroom argument under a regime in which participants are free to question what the data are data *for*, what theories, biases, and constraints are embedded in them, and therefore what the conditions are under which the data function as data. Similarly, "*there is no evidence for*" (an alternative hypothesis offered by a participant as an alternative way of explaining a fact) cannot by itself function as a legitimate *closer* of the public argument, not only because there are *many* concepts and theories in use that we have no evidence for without this constituting a prima facie reason to discard them but also because the very criterion "accept theory X only if you have evidence for it" becomes discussable and debatable.

Module 4. Poiesis, or the Production of Behavior

The fourth module aims to stimulate and develop the behavioral production capability of the integrator in the trainee by getting him or her to reengineer and reverse engineer his or her own behavior according to his or her introspected and considered aims. The basis of the module is once again part of the scholar's tool kit and consists of close, phenomenologically precise self-observation and analysis in controlled settings, followed by opportunities to produce new ways of interacting that are guided by a particular goal structure. Defensive interpersonal communication strategies, for instance, become subjects for personal behavioral reengineering when the defensive strategies of the trainee him- or herself are examined in a videotaped session in which they show up.

Because *poiesis* is about the holistic production of behavior that achieves a particular goal, such as turning a set of mutual misattributions into an open conversation, rather than about the satisfaction of certain behavioral constraints or the following of certain rule sets, the idea behind the module is to allow the trainee to become a *designer* of his or her own behavior, one that can purposefully shape his or her own behavior to self-determined ends. Because phenomena such as "conversations" or "meetings" more generally are complex interweavings of gestures, tones, words, sentences, and bodily movements, the module needs to make use of high-bandwidth behavioral playback devices—such as video recordings of the participants—in order to allow the would-be behavioral designer maximal access to the degrees of freedom of the design problem.

The module also enables a new way of teaching what has come to be known as rational-choice and rational-belief theory through the *imprinting* (as opposed to merely the *teaching*) of axiomatic, normative frameworks that are "tough to get across" by reference to rules alone (such as the axioms of rational choice and rational belief, which are cheerfully violated by students even after learning about them and, at least apparently, agreeing with their "correctness"; Dawes, 1998) . The axioms of rational choice and rational belief can be taught as ways of producing trading strategies that "sucker the suckers" and that avoid "being suckered oneself" in large, interactive trading or betting situations and internalized as *behavioral* axioms—rather than just as merely cognitive or analytical ones—if they emerge as the result of a process of *design*, rather than a process of proselytization or normative admonishments.

As part of the *articulation module*, basic intuitions about modeling beliefs and desires are first probed openly, and the rationale behind representing beliefs as measure-theoretic probabilities and utilities as (ordinal or cardinal) measures is allowed to emerge as an *engineering solution* to the problem of representing individual choice behavior in a way that optimally satisfies the concomitant modeler's needs for universalizability and goodness of fit in the face of many alternative phenomenologically grounded and plausible representations of belief and desire (see figure 3.2): the axes of the graph supply measures (in the analytic sense of the word) for the phenomenological descriptors of "belief states" and "desire states" that lie outside of the axes. The rational-choice framework appears then as a solution to the *problem of representation,* rather than as a normative rule set of questionable foundation and descent. What is essential here is that the trainee makes up his or her own mind about the utility of reducing various epistemic states and desire states for representational purposes to

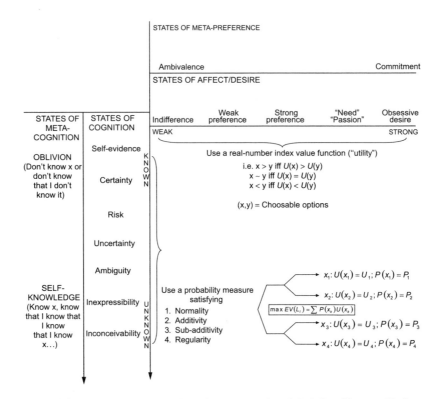

Figure 3.2. An Interactive, Engineering Approach to Modeling Human Choice

"degrees of belief" or probabilities and about the utility of reducing levels of desire, need, or preference to ordinal or cardinal "utilities."

Once the framework is established, the inverse problem of *inferring* personal probabilities from the observation of behavior—one of the core problems of management—is then used to introduce the Ramsey-de Finetti subjective probability framework (figure 3.3) as a way of extracting personal probabilities from observed choice behavior but, more relevantly, as a managerial *tool* for getting individuals to walk the talk by forcing them to lay implicit or explicit bets in accordance with their underlying beliefs and the probabilities attached to them.

Finally, the question of *Why follow the axioms of probability theory in forming judgments?* is not answered on purely normative grounds—"because it is the right way to think"—but rather via an interactive approach to the design of "money pumps," utility pumps, or Dutch books that extract a positive payoff with a high degree of reliability from traders whose personal probability measures *do not* obey the axioms of probability theory (figure 3.4). (This approach accords well with recent evidence that seasoned traders [List, 2004] do not exhibit many of the infamous "biases and fallacies" that are thought to unavoidably plague the human—and by extension the managerial—mind: they *learn* to be rational.) The logics of rational choice and rational belief, in this case, appear to be logics of action rather than merely cognitive logics: they are used to structure behavior. Thus a *poiesis* module can be understood as being fundamentally about the transformation of concepts into ontologies.

The modules we have introduced draw their life from the contemporary culture of the MBA classroom and academia. They develop skills that are—usually—understood by academics, because they are useful for the intellectually honest production of knowledge by means of analysis,

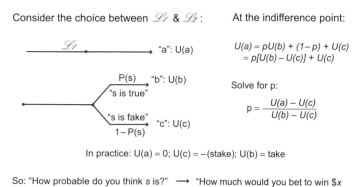

Figure 3.3. How to Extract Probabilities from People by Observing Their Choices

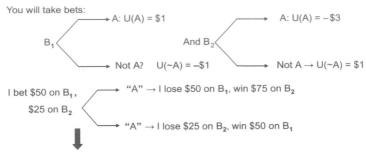

Event A = {S & P fall 5% or more next Monday}

You believe: P(A) = ½; P(not−A) = ¾

You will take bets:

B₁ → A: U(A) = $1

Not A? U(~A) = −$1

And B₂ → A: U(A) = −$3

Not A → U(~A) = $1

I bet $50 on B₁,
$25 on B₂

"A" → I lose $50 on B₁, win $75 on B₂

"A" → I lose $25 on B₂, win $50 on B₁

I make a sure profit of $25 by betting against you

Figure 3.4. A Money Pump: How to Extract a Positive Payoff (for Sure) from Someone Whose Beliefs Do Not Satisfy Probability Axioms (Lo, 2004)

experimentation, and quasi experimentation. They rely on generative semantics and grammars, models, metaphors, and representations that are the very foundations of theorizing in social science. They use basic models in the social sciences as engineering tools for designing more successful behaviors and as lenses for reformatting and reengineering the participant's behavior. Therefore, they accomplish the ends of a true practicum using the installed base of culture, technology, and task definitions that exist in business academia today.

Model II. The Design and Enactment of Communicative Spaces

The MBA classroom can be understood as a communication community, in which concepts are introduced, arguments that make use of them are deployed, theories resting on different arguments are presented, and counterarguments or comments are adduced, refined, and discussed. The arguments, ideas, counterarguments, facts, fictions, stories, histories, and forecasts that form the currency of the MBA communicative setting are based on different fundamental assumptions about human behavior and capabilities, different factual assumptions about a given situation, different forms of inference (deductive, inductive, abductive), different kinds of logic (modal, declarative, two-valued, many-valued, or fuzzy), different approaches to validation (falsificationist, justificationist), and different commitments to the overall logic of the conversation. The integrative repertoire of operations discussed next can be deployed and exercised in any MBA classroom that matches this basic communicative scenario.

Cultivating Canonical Skill Sets of Integrative Thinking
by Engineering the Communicative Space of the
MBA Classroom

The integrative thinker develops areas of *high-gain fit* or *synergy* among different models and theories. Even though no algorithmic rules can be given for how to achieve the integrative moment, the skills involved in understanding two or more incommensurable or conflicting models, theories, representations, or arguments can be not only named but also trained as part of MBA classroom discussions on any topic by focusing on the following fundamental operations—and the associated "operators."

Logical Auditing of Arguments   Understanding an argument rests minimally on understanding what kind of an argument it is, the kinds of inference the speaker considers to be valid, and the kinds of logic that he or she respects. Accordingly, the *logical audit* of arguments is a critical part of the integrator's skill set and can be understood as a discursive *prospecting tool:* it allows him or her to make sense of the structure(s) of someone else's (and his or her own) arguments. Developing a logical auditing module as part of classroom communication has two components: the *naming* of different kinds of arguments, inferences, and logics as they occur in the classroom and the *questioning* of the relative communicative validity, use, and value of these discursive structures to the speaker's argument.

Mapping and Understanding Kinds of Arguments   Arguments may be normative (what should be), descriptive (what is the case), and prescriptive (what should be or what one should do given what knows about what is the case). They can be empirical or nonempirical (including metaphysical and phenomenological arguments based on nonindependently verifiable introspection) with regard to their testability. The first step of a logical audit has to do with understanding the *grounds* for the claim to validity that the argument makes, and these two dimensions supply a set of grounds that can be uncovered and discussed. Obvious points of discussion include: how should one *value* strictly normative claims ("one should never use child labor to build one's products") vis-à-vis one another ("we have a *prima facie* contractual obligation to maximize the value of the equity of the firm"), vis-à-vis prescriptive claims ("given the socioeconomic situation of child laborers, it is in their best interest to have the option to work for very low wages"), and vis-à-vis cause-and-effect arguments based on descriptive claims ("if we pull out of Nigeria to protest unfair treatment of workers, another oil company will be invited to take our place")? How should metaphysical arguments (about the relative all-things-considered value of freedom, for instance) be valued vis-à-vis other metaphysical arguments (*for* the noninstrumental value of freedom or fairness) and vis-à-vis empirical arguments that do not seem to be consistent with the metaphysical position of the discussant ("is a commitment to fairness efficient?")?

Mapping and Understanding Kinds of Inference   How are arguments *put together?* What comprises the interstitial fabric that connects various claims together, claims to assumptions, and claims to possible sources of counterargument or empirical facts? Many areas of academia rely on both *deductive* (*modus ponens* and *modus tollens*) and *inductive* (extrapolating from a few cases to many cases, or from a few cases to an infinite number of cases) modes of inference, but practitioners (and students) often use *abductive* forms of inference (also called *inference to the best explanation,* which includes reasoning by analogy: "I saw (presumed) cause *C* produce actual effect *E* in situation *X,* which is like the current case with respect to relevant property set *R,* the current case exhibits cause *C,* therefore I expect effect *E* to obtain here as well.") This argument structure is frequent in classroom discussions, in which *"I saw this measure work in my firm in this situation"* often comes into conflict with *"I have experimental data that corroborates the opposite points of view."* Logical audits of an argument will call out such tensions, expose their logical structure, and get students to reflect on (1) ways of resolving them and (2) the relative value in the overall discussion that these interventions have. For instance, an argument may be said to "fall apart" if it rests on too large an inductive leap ("it worked once, it will always work") or if it rests on an abductive leap that admits of counterexamples ("putative causes *D, F* rather than presumed cause *C* could have caused effect *E* in the situation you refer to, and they are *not* present in the case at hand").

Mapping and Understanding Kinds of Logic   Science, including social science, is formulated in terms of declarative, first-order, two-valued ('true-false") deductive logic, occasionally augmented by an inductive logic (the probability axioms and Bayes's rule for updating prior probabilities in view of new data), and thus scientists *qua* scientists are naturally trained to audit arguments based on these kinds of different logics by retracing the steps that a communicator makes and pointing out with critical intent the steps that are not sanctioned by these logical rules. However, informal conversation exhibits other kinds of logics, such as *modal logics* (admitting possibilities, rather than facts and premises alone, as possible grounds for an argument), *many-valued logics* (four-valued logics in Eastern traditions, for instance, allowing both "both true and false" and "neither true nor false" in addition to "true" and "false" as truth operators), *fuzzy logics* (with truth values distributed between 0 and 1 but *not* obeying the probability axioms of independence, finite additivity, and subadditivity), and *higher-order logics* (admitting statements about statements and statements about statements about statements, in addition to statements about facts or states of the world). Logical auditing extends to the reconstruction of different *kinds of logic* in the communicative environment of the MBA classroom, consisting of identifying the kind of logic an argument makes use of and then considering the relative persuasiveness of the steps that make use of that kind of logic. For instance, what kind of evidential weight should be attached to what *could* happen in a particular case? What kind of weight should be given to statements that do not follow logically from the premises of the case discussion but are nevertheless useful in that they have a positive effect on the overall classroom discussion (such as shifts of inquiry, shifts of the problem statement from the realm of "what to do?" to the realm of "what ought to be done?")?

Conceptual Mapping: Understanding the
Conceptual Imagery of Arguments

Arguments are based on a conceptual machinery, or imagery, comprising the representations that that speaker makes use of when referring to the objects of the argument. A "firm" can be represented as a nexus of contracts in an agency theory course; as a concatenated set of variation, selection, and retention processes in a strategy class; as a communicative community in a class on organizational behavior; as a finite-state non-deterministic automaton in a case on the design and analysis of business plans; as a "brain" in an informal discussion of information flows and adaptation potential; as a network of affective relationships in a specialized discussion of emotion contagion; or as a computer in a discussion of operational and logistical optimization. Conceptual mapping refers to the process of explicitly identifying the deep-seated representations (including images and metaphors) of the objects of the classroom discussion and discussing (1) the relative validity and usefulness of these representations and (2) the possibilities of fit among two or more such representations. One can usefully ask: What does a representation of an organization as a nexus of contracts encourage you to think about or to do, and how is this different from the cognitive-behavioral repertoire associated with the "natural selection" model of an organization? What are the conditions under which one might switch conceptual frameworks, and how are these conditions related to the properties of the frameworks themselves?

Designing Inquiry: Sophisticated Falsificationist Validation and Critical Tests

As many researchers have discovered, the construction of new and useful concepts, arguments, and theories is greatly facilitated by the deployment of a validation technology such as falsificationism, based on (1) the specification of empirical tests for a particular theory or argument specifying logically possible conditions under which the theory or argument would turn out to be false; (2) the design of *actual* empirical tests, specifying *physically* possible conditions that *would* be observed if the theory or argument were *false;* (3) the critical evaluation of the empirical data on the basis of theories that may be embodied in its production, which involves critical tests of such theories as per (1) and (2); (4) the critical revision of the original theory and argument based on a considered interpretation of the results of the experiment and the critical evaluation of its results (and then the process begins again anew). Falsificationism can be developed and imprinted in the classroom not through the enunciation of a set of rules that one must follow but through the structuration of arguments and counterarguments in such a way as to make them both testable in principle and testable in fact, and the design of tests toward refutation rather than confirmation of arguments and theories advanced. Obviously productive discursive moves are: "How would you test that given the conditions at hand?" "How would you deal with this counterexample to the general statement embedded in your argument?" and "How would you respond to an empirical result that seems to disconfirm your idea?" Falsificationism, then, can be understood as a *communication technology,* a way of structuring communication with trainees which gets them to think about disconfirmation rather than confirmation, about testing rather than justifying, and about criticizing rather than buttressing arguments. Several steps are worth elaborating:

Discovering Epistemically Closed Networks of Beliefs and Arguments   This can be understood as an extension of logical auditing, aimed at figuring out the cognitive map corresponding to an argument (which can be reconstructed by asking, iteratively, *Why? In what sense? Under what conditions?*) of any particular proposition. Epistemically closed belief networks (or nets) exhibit the topological properties of circles (*circular arguments*), infinite strings (*infinite regress: believing A because B, B because C, C because D, D because...*) and recourse to absolute certainty ("*I just know it is so*") and, of course, combinations of the three structures (*"we believe the new technology does not work because, if it did, the competition would have implemented it by now, but the competition has not, which confirms our belief"*) and are closed in the sense that they are not responsive to counterarguments and the results of empirical tests. The first prong of a module aimed at training a "living falsificationism" concentrates on the discovery of the global structure of a participant's arguments.

Validating and Developing Challenges to Theories and General Arguments   Opening up epistemically closed belief nets to *counterargument* and disconfirming *data* can be accomplished by establishing a simple rule of conversation whereby valid counterarguments to general rules and principles *count so long as they are intersubjectively agreeable.* This is a tough rule, because "I know it will work here because I have seen it work in case X (which I was part of and you were not)" will not pass the intersubjectivity test.

Understanding and Promoting Challenges to Data   Data are not infallible: pure perception can be distorted by illusions and biases; the articulation of facts is not determined by perceptual experiences but is dependent on theories that can be embodied in conscious or unconscious centers of mental activity; failures of integrity work alongside failures of competence in the scientific community to produce distortions in what is presented as data relative to what is actually observed and articulated. Understanding the activity of researchers as a generalized form of inquiry meant to detect and correct instances of deception and self-deception and reflecting on the processes by which this is accomplished will help turn this practice into a process that can be transferred as part of the communicative setting of the MBA classroom. Turning falsificationism into a mode of argumentation and set of behavioral proclivities (rather than an algorithm or a dogma that focuses on "data for or against theory X") allows the critical, empirical investigation of what is presented as data alongside the critical investigation of what is presented as theory or general argument. As an example: a classroom argument does not need to stop at "here is an intersubjectively agreeable counterexample C to theory T, therefore let us abandon T," but can continue to "here is a set of general premises G that must ground acceptance of C as a data point; let us design or think of critical empirical tests of G." Simply observing and calling out the arguments and propositions that seem to clinch a point or end a discussion in the classroom will significantly help to turn the communicative experience into a laboratory for different forms of inquiry.

Designing a Logic of Selection for Arguments and Beliefs   As is evident from the preceding example, falsificationist logic does not have a natural or inevitable point of convergence or stopping rule. One can advance general argument A (capital structure of the firm matters because of the impact of agency costs on firm value); come up with a prima facie counterexample B (a small-cap public corporation with fragmented ownership has undergone many changes in capital structure with no change in value); show that B rests on general principles C and D (assumptions embedded in the researchers' methods), which themselves admit prima facie empirical falsifiers E and F (instances in which these methods reliably produced valid results); fail to find E but find F; agree that acceptance of F rests on general principle G; specify falsifiers H, I, J, K for.... Thus training in falsificationism as a practice must be carried out in the face of obvious temptations to produce a closure of the argument. Sophisticated reconstructions of falsificationism—such as that of Imre Lakatos (1970)—have recognized that scientists need to act like any other problem-solving organism and have produced a "doer's falsificationism" in which two or more incompatible models or theories are tested in parallel with critical—refutation-oriented—intent, and one is selected—provisionally—on the basis of how well it has fared in empirical testing, how empirically daring it was to begin with, and how novel and useful its empirical predictions are. Besides suggesting that model clash and model tension are valuable in themselves, sophisticated falsificationist approaches highlight the value of designing selection metrics for alternative models or theories, in which candidate variables include parsimony, empirical breadth, logical connectedness and coherence, and novelty of predictions. A discussion that focuses on the bases on which participants choose one general argument over another at the end of an argument will implicitly cultivate a sensitivity to the relevance and ubiquity of epistemic choice of the type that the sophisticated falsificationist frequently makes.

Communicative Ethics: Building and Sustaining a Running Metadialogue   The previous discussion points to the overarching role that a *communicative ethics* plays in the classroom, by which is meant the set of principles that one adheres to in making arguments and responding to arguments and counterarguments from others. Given that the integrative thinker must become an astute observer of his or her own thinking processes and that *thinking is a form of internal conversation,* the dialogue instantiated in the classroom can come to serve as a prototype or a template for internal processes of thinking, and explicitly addressing the rules and principles by which classroom conversation evolves in a way that conforms to those very rules and principles serves to instantiate a metadialogue that can be internalized as a process of thinking about thinking. What are the high-level elements of a discourse ethics that can be explicitly primed and encouraged and implicitly adhered to? Here are some fundamental questions that can be asked of any discursive situation and raised implicitly and explicitly in classroom discussions:

What Are the Dynamics of Achieving Logical Closure?   In particular: What happens when an argument is *not* carried to its logical conclusion or to some Archimedean point at which all participants are satisfied with deferring closure? What happens when a discussant argues premises A and also B, which, in conjunction with commonsense assumption C, implies *not-A?* What happens when a discussant claims to *not know the logical consequences* of a set of arguments F,G which he or she has just advanced?

What Are the Dynamics of Communicative Openness?   In particular: What happens when an argument is shut down by fiat in the classroom discussion or on the basis of a pragmatic interjection (time has run out or there is simply not enough energy left in the room to respond to it)? What happens when an argument is ruled out on the basis of the fact that it is nonempirical, without discussion of the agreeability of the general principle *accept only empirical arguments?*

What Are the Dynamics of Responsiveness?   In particular: What happens when a discussant answers to counterarguments X, Y to his argument V in ways that do not address the substantive import of X and Y to V, the respects, that is, in which X and Y are relevant to V?

In both of the approaches we have outlined earlier (models 1 and 2), we have rested on the thesis that current business academia could profitably focus on the imprinting of cognitive-behavioral modules—of "ways of being"—with which academics have firsthand experience, rather than merely on the transfer of information and knowledge structures—including "languages"—no matter how complex these may be. In what follows we shall buttress this claim with examples of successful educational programs that provide ontic-ontological bridges—bridges between concepts and behaviors—and argue that the creation of such bridges is critically important to the success of these programs and the associated disciplines.

The Value of the Ontic-Ontological Bridge: A Justification for the Cognitive-Behavioral Module Development Approach

To show the pedagogical power of cognitive-behavioral modules and operations, we consider now two educational programs that are often considered "successful" and argue that their achievements are related to the fact that they have successfully bridged the ontic-ontological gaps that separate theory from practice—essentially the aim of the modules we have described.

Successful Bridging of the Ontic-Ontological Gap Explains the Success of Medical Scientist and Financial Engineer Training Programs

The approach to professional development based on *cognitive-behavioral modules* common to both academics and practitioners can be understood as a foundational building block for successful medical scientist training programs and, more generally, for the success of professional, science-based medical training.[1] Here is how: conventional medicine has achieved an effective monopoly over the technologies of investigating and intervening in human disease processes through the successful *rapprochement* between science and practice (Starr, 1982; Abbott, 1988), which has led *both* to the embodiment of a scientific ethos in practice and to a practically relevant problem base for medical science. In turn, this rapprochement has led to both greater practical relevance for medical science and greater scientific legitimacy for medical practice.

How is this accomplished? If we map the deep structures of behavior and cognition associated with clinical activity and examine the logic of argumentation (declarative, modal), the allowable forms of inference (deductive, inductive, abductive), and the basic logics of explanation (causal, functional, intentional), we find that the process that takes the clinician from recognition of symptoms through the articulation of a differential diagnosis and the prescription of tests aimed at discriminating among the various possibilities to the prescription of a course of action (or of a set of potential courses of action) smoothly incorporates the basic

---

1. Note that, unlike Bennis and O'Toole, we do not advocate that MBA programs should adopt elements from a medical education nor maintain that medical education is successful without qualifications in producing health care professionals (see the Introduction). Rather, we are pointing out the medical scientist training program as a successful model for the integration of the skills of the instructor and researcher with the skills of the practitioner, such that the questions "Why should I learn this?" and "How is this relevant?" do not often come up in the post-basic-science years of medical training. It *is* the case, however, that medical practice has used the legitimacy that science enjoys currently in conjunction with its close association with scientific methods to successfully establish a monopoly over the means for investigating and treating illness. Whether or not this economic success also corresponds to success at treating illness is something we will not know until we devise alternative approaches to minting physicians.

cognitive-behavioral building blocks of the tough-minded scientist (featuring an emphasis on deduction, logical closure, empirical testability, refutability, and *de facto* refutation as a way of discriminating among hypotheses) and seamlessly interleaves it with the elements of a designer's tool kit (modal logic alongside declarative logic; abductive inference alongside inductive and deductive inference; intentional and functional explanations alongside causal ones).

The contribution of the "scientific mind-set" to the overall production function of the medical scientist is clear and valuable. Its integration into the overall production function of the medical education process (i.e., the process by which the medical-scientific complex produces physicians) is accomplished without—at any point—having to explicitly address the problem of legitimacy or relevance because the "logic of science" is (already) part of the logic of practice and does not need independent justification as a guarantor of legitimate or usable knowledge (figure 3.5). To the trained physician, the logic that produces differential diagnosis sets and laboratory tests designed to select among them is not a theoretical logic—it is not what currently the probability axioms are to most MBA

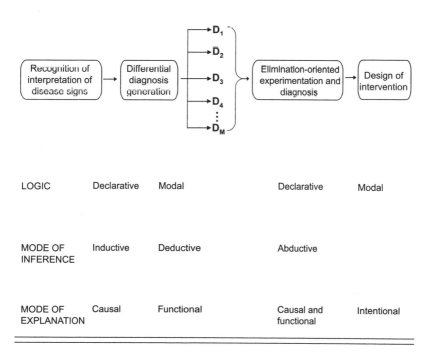

Figure 3.5. The Physician-Scientist Training Program: Deep-Structure Analysis

students: a seemingly sensible theory that has limited use—rather, it is *lived*. Logic thus conceived is an *activity*, not merely a set of principles.

The same kind of deep-structure analysis can be used to explain why finance training "works" as an educational experience within MBA programs and, more recently, in dedicated programs for the training of financial engineers and scientists. We note that both critics of the MBA (the most notable of which we discussed earlier on) and *their* critics (De Angelo, De Angelo, & Zimmerman, 2004) often agree that finance scholarship produces useful, transferable, and actually transferred knowledge to MBA students, knowledge whose "market value" is both measurable and significant. Why? Because, we argue, finance training rests on a set of problem statements accepted by both academics and practitioners, an unproblematic ontology—a set of objects that "matter" and "are real"— and a self-reinforcing mechanism for belief validation and selection, one that penalizes counternormative ways of making bets (figure 3.6) and that is accepted by academics. Unlike research in organizational behavior, strategy, and marketing, in which conceptual schemata are deployed in understanding managerial phenomena that do not have, prima facie, much in common with the schemata that the studied managers use to make sense of their own predicaments, the ontology of finance *supplies* the conceptual schemata of finance scholars, which, in turn, directly

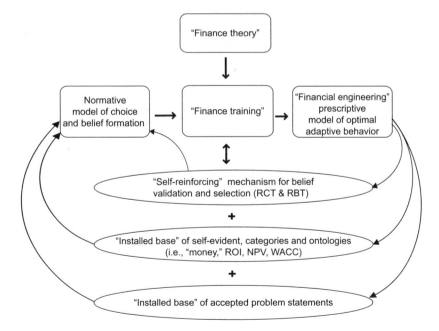

Figure 3.6. Why Finance Training "Works"

address the problems that traders and investors face *in the language in which they address those problems.* There is, then, no schism, in finance, between the ontic and the ontological dimension; finance scholars have a large "installed base" of problems that are ontically tailored to their solution concepts and theories.

This installed base of problems, objects, and epistemologies makes up the normative base of finance theory. Training in financial engineering not only gives one *point prescriptions* for action but also inculcates a *way of generating* such prescriptions and, even more important, a way of articulating problem statements by the imprinting of a mind-set that (similarly to the medical training model) integrates elements of "science" with elements of "design." The "installed base of self-evident foundational knowledge and practices" allows the discipline of finance to transfer its "science" into "practice" seamlessly and to claim for itself the value associated with the inculcation of science-based skills that are already *in practice.*

This example, like the previous one, is *not* meant to encourage other managerial disciplines to emulate finance theory via the narrowing of their axiomatic bases and a purely technical and reductionist approach to problem solving. Indeed, they cannot, because the ontological fit between the activities of researchers and the activities of their students does not exist in any other managerial field. Rather, it should be understood as explaining why other disciplines should *not* attempt it: they lack the unproblematic ontological and epistemological "installed base." The example is, rather, meant to highlight the importance of developing transferable and useful cognitive behavioral modules and operations. As the successful "scientificization" of medicine suggests, it *is* possible to design the tool kit of the scientist into a practitioner-oriented training program—and thus to impact the very definition of the MBA and of the value the degree brings to the individual and the organization. But for business academia in general, this transfer occurs at the level of communicative practice and methodological know-how rather than at the lower levels of technical know-what and practical know-how. The applied social scientist's methods of inquiry and modes of communicating about its results are, we posit, more valuable than the "theories" and "data" that are the usual end-points of inquiry and dialogue.

4

Epilogue

A Reconstructive Summary

We have made several moves in this book, and it is worth reconstructing the argument in a compact form, which will allow us to bring together its various components and see how they relate to each other.

We started out discussing recent critiques of the MBA as a program of training and development for managers and argued that many of the critiques do not recognize the *selection* value of the MBA, its value as a selection mechanism or filter that picks out individuals with high potential for management positions based on relatively powerful predictors of performance, such as general intelligence and conscientiousness. Not recognizing this value leads, in the cases of many critics, to difficulties in explaining the high value that markets continue to attach to MBA graduates, in spite of the fact that the MBA as a development program faces problems and dilemmas that they competently call out. In particular, we argued:

> (SV-MBA) The MBA has a significant, demonstrable, and robust value to prospective employers as a *selection mechanism*, which is not entirely separable from its function as a *development* program.

When the need for a selection filter is addressed—as is the case with Henry Mintzberg's critique—the selection function is delegated to the employer organizations, which creates the situation of subcontracting to the customer a function that the customer is willing to pay for. Indeed, it is not clear that the organizational "rat race" *can* by itself efficiently fulfill the selection function that the MBA degree provides, because the selection task adds the most value to organizations precisely at the point in the managerial life cycle—talented, ambitious 30-year-olds—at which the organizational pyramid is the widest and the selection function would be most costly to perform.

The realization of the selection value of the MBA has two important corollaries. The first is that, even if they are useless as development and training programs, MBA programs can be understood to provide a significant and stable economic benefit to the "end users" that should allow MBA educators significant room to design and experiment with new approaches to development. There is no reason for hysteria or panic, but there is a good reason for undertaking innovation-driven design, as—the point of several critics—the *development* value of the program is currently questionable. The second corollary is that once selection is understood as part of the function of the MBA, the selection criteria and metrics can themselves be redesigned and optimized. But to what end?

We argued that a missing component of current critiques is a vision of what we called the "high-value decision maker"—of the objective function of the MBA program's function—and that the task of articulating such a vision cannot fall to markets, as they are concept takers, not concept makers; selectors, not articulators; information processors, not designers. It is only relative to such a vision that the all-things-considered value of the MBA can be estimated and proactive design and prototyping efforts can proceed. Otherwise, we are left with ascertaining only *ex post* the effects of any particular curricular and structural change and inferring long-term value from immediate short-term returns alone—a difficult proposition for an institutional structure with the time scales for change of academia.

We then articulated a vision for the high-value decision maker of the future and called him or her an *integrator*, who can produce constructive reconciliations of tensions among different models, theories, beliefs, and ways of knowing, acting, and being—to the end of enabling successful action in prototypically "postmodern" organizational environments. We argued that:

> (INT-V) The integrator's production function is valuable, not subcontractible, and nonalgorithmic.

We contrasted the integrator's production function with the production function of the optimizer, whose task is to push the operations of the organization to the Pareto frontier of trade-offs among different combinations of inputs. By contrast, we argued that the integrator pushes outward that very Pareto frontier that the optimizer is trying to reach, and we illustrated the integrator's production function with examples and with a phenomenological analysis of the tasks it comprises. These tasks, we argued, embody *tacit* knowledge, know-how rather than know-what; they are not reducible to an algorithmic representation; and they instantiate the ability of managers and talented actors more generally to resolve, dissolve, or cut through in action as well as thinking fundamental problems that have sprouted at the very core of mainstream scientific theorizing over the past hundred years. *The integrator solves through action what the narrow specialist can often not solve even in theory.*

Given this foundation, we attempted to articulate a characteristic profile of the integrator to the end of augmenting and refining the selection filter that an MBA program can provide and argued for extending the "institutional" core that includes conscientiousness and general intelligence to include measures of openness in combination with an executive function that allows the integrator to manage his or her internal affective and cognitive processes to the end of being able to contemplate different possible worlds while retaining the ability to function and to command him- or herself to act in spite of an inherent and inherently irresolvable state of practical ambiguity. Accordingly, we argued for an expansion and refinement of the selection metric that MBA programs currently use and that has never been consciously optimized.

We next asked: Can business academia deliver a development program more likely to cultivate the high-value decision maker of the future than is currently the case? We projected various components of the integrator's production function onto the intellectual and performative landscape of business academia and found that, although the value of the *know-what* imparted by business schools may be in many cases low, the value of the *know-how* that business school academics can provide is undervalued and can be significantly increased by recognizing and amplifying powerful trends that have emerged in the field over the past 20 years. These trends can be used to create "a new kind of science" based on the recognition of the disciplinary straitjackets imposed on academic business thinking by the methodological and conceptual straitjackets of tributary basic sciences such as economics, psychology, and sociology and the emancipation of the conceptual foundations and methodological practices of business academia from their currently more "respectable" intellectual precursors. Specifically, we argued:

> (KH-KW) Business academics know *how* to perform tasks of greater value to the integrator than that of the knowledge structures they can transfer in the classroom through traditional methods.

We pointed as examples to the similarities between the falsification-ist ethos of scientific inquiry and the refutation-oriented logic of sound model testing. We pointed to the importance of the skill of *articulating* models for a particular phenomenon or event that business scholars engage with as a matter of course and that integrators must master and to the engineering of reflective and open communicative spaces, which are as important to the pursuit of new theories and models as they are to the management of difficult situations of conflict among incommensurable models of the world, ways of knowing, and standards of reasoning.

We proceeded on the assumption that:

> (KH-MT) Relevant, valuable *know-how* can be successfully *transferred* through discursive interaction and *mimetic* imprinting.

and articulated a set of cognitive-behavioral modules and basic operations—both of them vehicles for the transfer of valuable *know-how* from scholars to future managers—and showed that the development and cultivation of such modules can be pursued either through the design of thinking and action design labs specifically designed to highlight the performative dimension of academic knowledge creation and validation or through the design of communicative spaces in MBA classrooms that are aimed at implicitly training the relevant dispositions and capabilities without regard to substantive context.

To buttress our argument for a redesign of the training experience of the MBA focused on the performative dimension of knowledge, rather than the representational one, we showed that prototypically "successful" training programs such as those for medical scientists or financial engineers are always already based on an identification of the ontic with the ontological realms—on a careful union of the embodied skills involved in doing with those involved in thinking about doing—suggesting the following simple design precept whose utility may go far beyond the application we have examined here:

> (OO-TP) Whenever possible, bring the *ontic* and *onto-logical* dimensions of training together in the same elements of a training program.

Or, to paraphrase Heinz von Foerster's aesthetical imperative, "If you want to learn how to think, you must first learn how to act" (von Foerster, 2003).

Problems that we raised up front with critiques of the MBA will, by now, have been addressed. We see, for instance, why it is not sufficient to claim that MBA "theories" are "bad for business," as Ghoshal does: because of the very epistemological indeterminacies that allow normative assumptions to be smuggled into descriptive frameworks, there is no line of causation that goes from understanding the world through the lens of a particular concept and a particular course of action. However, the freedom to escape the illusion of such a line has to be won through the instantiation of a skill, and this skill is instantiated both in the integrator's tool kit and in the practice of intellectually honest scholarship. We also see why it is not sufficient to point to problems with the MBA vis-à-vis "role models" such as medicine or law, which supposedly effect a more successful melding of theory and practice. What is required is an understanding of the ways in which other training programs effect this melding, so that what is "imported" is not a potentially epiphenomenal institutional structure in which practitioners get to teach (and vice versa) but the *real thing:* an understanding of the mechanisms by which concepts, objects, and activities come together in training. We see, finally, why institutionalization and professionalization of management by themselves along the lines that can be drawn out by current business academics is an incomplete solution. It must be augmented by a vision that articulates the value of academic know-how to the cognitive-behavioral repertoire of the high-value decision maker. Only then can we claim that imprinting has a value that lies beyond the repetitive perpetuation—and perpetual return—of the same.

References

Abbott, A. G. (1988). *The system of professions*. Chicago: University of Chicago Press.

Abelson, R. (1986). Beliefs are like possessions. *Journal for the Theory of Social Behaviour, 16*(3), 223–250.

Abelson, R., Frey, K., & Gregg, A. (2004). *Experiments with people: Revelations from social psychology*. Mahwah, NJ: Erlbaum.

Albert, H. (1985). *Treatise on critical reason*. Princeton, NJ: Princeton University Press.

Anderlini, L., & Felli, L. (1994). Undescribable states of nature: A theory of incomplete contracts. *Quarterly Journal of Economics, 109*, 1089–1145.

Anderson, J. R. (1978). Arguments concerning representations for mental imagery. *Psychological Review, 85*, 249–277.

Apel, K. (1980). *Towards a transformation of philosophy*. London: Routledge & Kegan Paul.

Argyris, C. (1980). Some limitations of the case method: Experiences in a management development program. *Academy of Management Review, 5*(2), 291–298.

Argyris, C. (1993a). *Knowledge for action: A guide to overcoming barriers to organizational change*. San Francisco: Jossey-Bass.

Argyris, C. (1993b). *On organizational learning*. Cambridge, MA: Harvard University Press.

Argyris, C., & Schon, D. (1978). *Organizational learning: A theory of action perspective*. Reading, MA: Addison-Wesley.

Aronson, E. (1993). *The social animal*. Hillside, NJ: Erlbaum.

Astley, W. G., & Zammuto, R. F. (1992). Organization science, managers, and language games. *Organization Science, 3*, 443–460.

Audi, R. (1988). *Epistemology: An introduction.* New York: Cambridge University Press.

Barnard, C. (1968). *The functions of the executive.* Cambridge, MA: Harvard University Press.

Baum, J. A. C., & Dobbin, F. (2000). Doing interdisciplinary research in strategic management—without a paradigm war. *Advances in Strategic Management, 17,* 389–410.

Bayes, T. (1763). An essay towards solving a problem in the doctrine of chances. *Philosophical Transactions of the Royal Society, 53,* 370–418.

Bazerman, M. (1995/2002). *Judgment in managerial decision making.* New York: Wiley.

Beardsley, S. C., Johnson, B. C., & Manyika, J. M. (2006). Competitive advantage from better interactions. *McKinsey Quarterly, No. 2,* 52–63.

Bell, D., Raiffa, H., & Tversky, A. (1988). *Decision making: Normative, descriptive and prescriptive approaches.* New York: Cambridge University Press.

Bennis, W., & O'Toole, J. (2005). How business schools lost their way. *Harvard Business Review, 83*(5), 96–104.

Berlinski, D. (2001). *The advent of the algorithm.* New York: Basic Books.

Burt, R. S. (1999). The network structure of social capital. In R. I. Sutton and B. M. Staw (Eds.), *Research in organizational behavior.* Greenwich, CT: JAI Press.

Dawes, R. (1988). *Rational choice in an uncertain world.* Orlando, FL: Harcourt Brace Jovanovich.

Dawes, R. M. (1998). Behavioral decision making. In D. T. Gilbert, S. T. Fiske, & G. Lindzey (Eds.), *Handbook of social psychology* (4th ed., Vol. 1, pp. 497–548). Boston: McGraw-Hill.

De Angelo, H., De Angelo, L., & Zimmerman, J. (2005). *What's really wrong with U.S. business schools?* Working paper, University of Rochester, Social science Research Network paper 766404, available at www.ssrn.com

De Finetti, B. (1937). La prevision: Ses lois logigues, ses sources subjectives. *Annales de L'Institut Henri Poincare, 7,* 1–68.

Dreyfus, H. L, & Dreyfus, L. E. (1986). *Mind over machine: The power of human intuition and expertise in the era of computers.* New York: Free Press.

Duhem, P. (1989). *The aim and structure of physical theory.* Princeton, NJ: Princeton University Press. (Original work published 1913)

Elster, J. (1982). Marxism, functionalism, game theory: The case for methodological individualism. *Theory and Society, 11*(4), 453–482.

Elster, J. (1989). *Nuts and bolts for the social sciences.* New York: Cambridge University Press.

Eysenck, H. (1995). *Genius: The natural history of creativity.* Cambridge, U.K.: Cambridge University Press.

Frank, R. H., Gilovich, T., & Regan, D. T. (1993). Does studying economics inhibit cooperation? *Journal of Economic Perspectives, 7*(2), 159.

Friedman, M. (1953). The methodology of positive economics. In M. Friedman, *Essays in positive economics.* Chicago: University of Chicago Press.

Friedman, T. (2005). *The world is flat.* New York: Basic Books.

Gallese, V., Keysers, C., & Rizzolatti, G. (2004). A unifying view of the basis of social cognition. *Trends in Cognitive Sciences, 8,* 396–403.

Gardner, H. (1993). *Frames of mind: The theory of multiple intelligences.* New York: Basic Books.

Gemes, K. (1997). Inductive skepticism and the probability calculus: I. Popper and Jeffreys on induction and the probability of law-like universal generalizations. *Philosophy of Science, 64,* 113–130.

Ghoshal, S. (2005). Bad management theories are destroying good management practices. *Academy of Management Learning and Education, 4*(1), 75–91.

Gigerenzer, G. (1991). From tools to theories: A heuristic of discovery in cognitive psychology. *Psychological Review,* 98, 254–267.

Gigerenzer, G., & Goldstein, D. G. (1996). Mind as computer: The birth of a metaphor. *Creativity Research Journal, 9,* 131–144.

Gigerenzer, G., Swijtink, Z., Porter, T., Daston, L., Beatty, J., & Krüger, L. (1989). *The empire of chance: How probability changed science and everyday life.* Cambridge, UK: Cambridge University Press.

Gilovich, T. (1991). *How we know what isn't so: The fallibility of human reason in everyday life.* New York: Free Press.

Goldberg, L. R. (1992). The development of markers for the Big Five factor structure. *Psychological Assessment, 4,* 26–42.

Goodman, N. (1974). *Fact, fiction, and forecast.* Cambridge, MA: Harvard University Press.

Gottfredson, L. S. (1997). Why g matters: The complexity of everyday life. *Intelligence, 24,* 79–132.

Greenwald, A. T. (1980). The totalitarian ego. *American Psychologist, 35,* 603–618.

Grice, H. P. (1975). Logic and conversation. In P. Cole & J. Morgan (Eds.), *Syntax and semantics* (Vol. 3). New York: Academic Press.

Grove, A. (1996). *Only the paranoid survive.* New York: Random House.

Habermas, J. (1984). *The theory of communicative action.* Trans. Thomas McCarthy. Boston: Beacon Press.

Habermas, J. (1993). *Moral consciousness and communicative action.* Cambridge, MA: MIT Press.

Hacking, I. (1984). *Why does language matter to philosophy?* New York: Cambridge University Press.

Heath, C., & Tversky, A. (1991). Preference and belief: Ambiguity and competence in choice under uncertainty. *Journal of Risk and Uncertainty, 4,* 177–212.

Heidegger, M. (1973). *The question concerning technology.* Trans. Joan Stambaugh. New York: Harper.

Heidegger, M. (1996). *Being and time.* Trans. Joan Stambaugh. Albany: State University of New York Press. (Original work published 1927)

Hempel, C. (1941). *Philosophy of natural science.* New York: Prentice Hall.

Higgins, D., Peterson, J. B., Pihl, N., & Lee, A. (2006). Prefrontal cognitive ability, intelligence, Big Five personality, and the prediction of advanced academic and workplace performance. *Journal of Personality and Social Psychology,* forthcoming.

Homer Dixon, T. (2000). *The ingenuity gap: How can we solve the problems of the future?* New York: Knopf.

Howson, C. (1995). Theories of probability. *British Journal for the Philosophy of Science, 46,* 218–239.

Howson, C. (2001). The logic of Bayesian probability. In D. Corfield & J. Williamson (Eds.), *Foundations of Bayesianism.* Boston: Kluwer Academic.

Ickes, W. (Ed.). (1997). *Empathic accuracy.* New York: Guilford Press.

Jensen, M. C., & Meckling, W. H. (1976). Theory of the firm: Managerial behavior, agency costs, and ownership structure. *Journal of Financial Economics, 3*(4), 305–360.

Johnson, B., Manyika, J. M., & Yee, L. A. (2005). The next revolution in interactions. *McKinsey Quarterly, 4,* 20–34.

Kahneman, D., & Lovallo, D. (1994). Timid choices and bold forecasts. In R. P. Rumelt, D. Schendel, & D. J. Teece (Eds.), *Fundamental issues in strategy: A research agenda.* Boston: Harvard Business School Press.

Kahneman, D., & Tversky, A. (1982). Subjective probability: A judgment of representativeness. In D. Kahneman, P. Slovic, & A. Tversky (Eds.), *Judgment under uncertainty: Heuristics and biases.* New York: Cambridge University Press.

Kelley, H. (1973). The process of causal attribution. *American Psychologist, 28,* 107–128.

Klein, G. (1998). *Sources of power.* Cambridge, MA: MIT Press.

Kreps, D. (1990). Corporate culture and economic theory. In J. Alt & K. Shepsle (Eds.), *Perspectives in positive political economy.* New York: Cambridge University Press.

Kruglanski, A. W., & Webster, D. M. (1996). Motivated closing of the mind: "Seizing" and "freezing." *Psychological Review, 103,* 263–283.

Kuhn, T. (1962). *The structure of scientific revolutions.* Chicago: University of Chicago Press.

Lakatos, I. (1970). Falsification and the methodology of scientific research programmes. In I. Lakatos & A. Musgrave (Eds.), *Criticism and the growth of knowledge.* Cambridge, UK: Cambridge University Press.

Lakoff, G., & Johnson, M. (1999). *Philosophy in the flesh: The embodied mind and its challenge to Western thought.* New York: Basic Books.

Langer, E. J. (2000). Private communication.

Laplace, P. S. (1966). *Mécanique céleste.* Trans. by N. Bowditch. New York: Chelsea. (Original work published 1799)

Lipman, B. L. (1991). How to decide how to decide how to…: Modeling limited rationality. *Econometrica, 59,* 1105–1125.

List, J. A. (2004). Neoclassical theory versus prospect theory: Evidence from the marketplace. *Econometrica, 72,* 615–625.

Lyotard, J.-F. (1979). *The postmodern condition.* Minneapolis: University of Minnesota Press.

Mannheim, K. (1989). *Ideology and utopia.* Chicago: Northwestern University Press. (Original work published 1935)

March, J. G., Sproull, L., & Tamuz, M. (1991). Learning from samples of one or fewer. *Organization Science, 2,* 1–13.

McKelvey, B. (1997). Quasi-natural organization science. *Organization Science, 8,* 352–380.

McKelvey, B. (1999). Avoiding complexity catastrophe in co-evolutionary pockets: Strategies for rugged landscapes. *Organization Science, 10,* 294–321.

Merritt, J. (2003). What's an MBA really worth? *BusinessWeek,* September 11.

Miller, D. (1994). Critical rationalism: A restatement and defence. Chicago: Open Court.

Mintzberg, H. (2004). *Managers, not MBAs: A hard look at the soft practice of managing and management development.* San Francisco: Berrett-Koehler.

Moldoveanu, M. C. (2000). Foundations of the open society: Discourse ethics and the logic of inquiry. *Journal of Socio-Economics, 29,* 403–442.

Moldoveanu, M. C. (2001). Epistemology in action: A framework for understanding organizational due diligence processes. In C.W. Choo & N. Bontis (Eds.), *The strategic management of intellectual capital and organizational knowledge.* New York: Oxford University Press.

Moldoveanu, M. C. (2002). Language, games, and language games. *Journal of Socio Economics, 31,* 233–251.

Moldoveanu, M. C. (2005). An intersubjective measure of organizational complexity: A new approach. In K. A. Richardson (Ed.), *Managing organizational complexity: Philosophy, theory and application.* Greenwich: Information Age.

Moldoveanu, M. C., & Baum, J. A. C. (2002). Contemporary debates in organizational epistemology. In J. A. C. Baum (Ed.), *The Blackwell companion to organizations* (pp. 733–751). Malden, MA: Blackwell.

Moldoveanu, M. C., & Langer, E. J. (2002). False memories of the future: A critique of the application of probabilistic reasoning to the study of cognitive processes. *Psychological Review, 109,* 358–375.

Moldoveanu, M. C., & Martin, R. L. (2001). Agency theory and the design of efficient governance mechanisms. Paper prepared for the Joint Committee on Corporate Governance, Canadian Institute of Chartered Accountants White Paper 01–2001, available from www.cica.org

Moldoveanu, M. C., & Singh, J. V. (2003). The evolutionary metaphor: A synthetic framework for the study of strategic organization. *Strategic Organization, 1,* 439–449.

Morgan, G. (1997). *Images of organization.* Hillsdale, NJ: Sage.

Munger, C. (1998). Wordly wisdom re-visited. *Outstanding Investor Digest, 13,* 1–2.

Muraven, M. and Baumeister, R. F. (2000). Self-regulation and depletion of limited resources: Does self-control resemble a muscle? *Psychological Review, 126,* 247–259.

Nickerson, R. S. (1996). Ambiguities and unstated assumptions in probabilistic reasoning. *Psychological Bulletin, 120,* 410–433.

Niilinuto, I. (1998). Verisimilitude: The next phase. *British Journal for the Philosophy of Science, 49,* 111–134.

Nisbett, R., & Ross, L. (1980). *Human inference.* Hillsdale, NJ: Erlbaum.

Nozick, R. (2001). *Invariances: The structure of the objective world.* Cambridge, MA: Belknap Press.

Pfeffer, J. (1981). *Power in organizations.* Cambridge, MA: Ballinger.

Pfeffer, J. (1993). Barriers to the advance of organizational science: Paradigm development as a dependent variable. *Academy of Management Review, 18,* 599–620.

Pfeffer, J. (2006). The end of business schools? Presentation to the Future of the MBA conference for business school deans and their critics, March 26–27, 2006, Desautels Centre for Integrative Thinking, Rotman School of Management, University of Toronto.

Pfeffer, J., & Fong, C. (2002). The end of business schools? Less success than meets the eye. *Academy of Management Learning and Education, 1,* 78–95.

Pfeffer, J., & Fong, C. (2004). The business school "business": Some lessons from the U.S. experience. *Journal of Management Studies, 41*(8), 1501–1520.

Popper, K. (1959). The logic of scientific discovery. London: Hutchinson.

Popper, K. (1961). The poverty of historicism (2nd ed.). London: Routledge.

Popper, K. R. (1973). *Objective knowledge.* London: Routledge.

Popper, K. R. (1979). *Knowledge and the body-mind problem.* London: Routledge.

Popper, K. R. (1983). *Realism and the aim of science.* London: Routledge.

Porter, L. W., & McKibbin, L. E. (1988). *Management education and development: Drift or thrust into the 21st century?* New York: McGraw-Hill.

Porter, M. (1996, November–December). What is strategy? *Harvard Business Review.*

Quine, W. v. O. (1969a). *Natural kinds.* In W. v. O. Quine, *Ontological relativity and other essays.* New York: Columbia University Press. (Original work published 1951)

Quine, W. v. O. (1969b). *Ontological relativity.* In W. v. O. Quine, *Ontological relativity and other essays.* New York: Columbia University Press. (Original work published 1961)

Ramsey, F. P. (1931). Truth and probability. In R. B. Braithwaite (Ed.), *The foundations of mathematics.* London: Routledge & Kegan Paul.

Roethlisberger, F. J. (1980). *The elusive phenomena: An autobiographical account of my work in the field of organizational behavior at the Harvard Business School.* Ed. G. Lombard. Cambridge, MA: Harvard University Press.

Roth, A. E. (2003). The economist as engineer: Game theory, experimentation, and computation as tools for design economics. *Econometrica, 70,* 1341–1378.

Saloner, G. (1994). *Game theory and strategic management.* In R. P. Rumelt, D. E. Schendel, & D. J. Teece (Eds.), *Fundamental issues in strategy.* Boston: Harvard Business School Press. (Original work published 1991)

Saul, J. R. (1992). *Voltaire's bastards: The dictatorship of reason in the West.* New York: Random House.

Savage, L. (1972). *Foundations of statistics.* New York: Dover. (Original work published 1954)

Schelling, T. (1984). The mind as a consuming organ. Presentation to Working Group on Rationality, Maison des sciences de L'Homme (Paris), reprinted in J. Elster (Ed.), *The Multiple Self.* New York: Cambridge University Press.

Schwarz, N. (1988). Accessible context and accessibility experiences: The interplay of declarative and experiential information in judgment. *Personality and Social Psychology Review, 2,* 87–99.

Schwarz, N., & Bless, H. (1992). Constructing reality and its alternatives: Assimilation and contrast effects in social judgment. In L. L. Martin & A. Tesser (Eds.), *The construction of social judgment.* Hillsdale, NJ: Erlbaum.

Schwarz, N., Strack, F., & Mai, H. P. (1991). Assimilation and contrast effects in part-whole question sequences: A conversational logic analysis. *Public Opinion Quarterly, 55,* 3–23.

Schwenk, R. (1984). Cognitive simplification processes in strategic decision making. *Strategic Management Journal, 5,* 111–128.

Searle, J. (2001). *Rationality in action.* Cambridge, MA: MIT Press.

Simon, H. (1986). The science of design: Creating the artificial. In H. A. Simon (Ed.), *The sciences of the artificial* Cambridge, MA: MIT Press. (Original work published 1969)

Simon, H. A. (1990). Invariants of human behavior. *Annual Review of Psychology, 41,* 1–19.

Sloan, A. P. (1964). *My years with General Motors.* New York: Doubleday.

Starr, T. (1982). *The social transformation of American medicine.* Cambridge, MA: Harvard University Press.

Sternberg, R. J. (1985). *Beyond IQ: A triarchic theory of human intelligence.* New York: Cambridge University Press.

Topkis, D. M. (1998). *Supermodularity and complementarity.* Princeton, NJ: Princeton University Press.

Tversky, A., & Kahneman, D. (1980). Causal schemas in judgments under uncertainty. In M. Fishbein (Ed.), *Progress in social psychology.* Hillsdale, NJ: Erlbaum.

Tversky, A., & Kahneman, D. (1982). Judgment of and by representativeness. In D. Kahneman, P. Slovic, & A. Tversky (Eds.), *Judgment under uncertainty: Heuristics and biases.* New York: Cambridge University Press.

Tversky, A., & Kahneman, D. (1986). Rational choice and the framing of decisions. *Journal of Business, 59,* S251–278.

Van Maanen, J. (1995). Style as theory. *Organization Science, 6*(1), 133–143.

von Foerster, H. (2003). On constructing a reality. In H. von Foerster (Ed.), *Understanding understanding: Essays on cybernetics and cognition.* New York: Springer.

von Mises, L. (1939). *Probability, statistics, and truth.* London: Unwin Allen.

Weber, M. (1991). Objectivity and value. In M. McIntyre & M. Martin (Eds.), *Philosophy of the social sciences.* Cambridge, MA: MIT Press. (Original work published 1911)

Wegner, D. T. (1994). Ironic processes of mental control. *Psychological Review, 101,* 34–52.

Index